Women *of* Worth

Bethany Frymire, CFP®, CKA®

HARVEST HOUSE PUBLISHERS
EUGENE, OREGON

Other Scripture versions used in this book are listed at the back of the book.

The names and identifying information of clients and other parties as appropriate in this book have been changed to protect their privacy and respect their confidentiality.

Trust and investment management accounts and services offered by Blue Trust, Inc. are not insured by the FDIC or any other federal government agency, are not deposits or other obligations of, nor guaranteed by, any bank or bank affiliate, and are subject to investment risk, including possible loss of the principal amount invested. The information found in this book is intended to be educational in nature and may not be applicable to your current portfolio or financial strategy. You should not rely on any of the information as authoritative or a substitute for the exercise of your own skill and judgment in making any investment or other decision. All information is current as of the original date of this book and subject to change. These clients' experiences may not be representative of the experience of other clients. Their experiences are also not indicative of future performance or success. Blue Trust and its employees do not provide legal or accounting advice or service. Work with your attorney or accounting professional for such services. At Blue Trust, we are committed to safeguarding client information provided to us. To learn more, visit www.BlueTrust.com/regulatory. We recommend that individuals consult with a professional familiar with their particular situation for advice concerning specific investments, accounting, tax, and legal matters or other matters before taking any action. All investment involves risk and should be carefully considered.

Cover design by Kyler Dougherty
Cover images © Vik_Y, kritdarat Atsadayuttmetee / Getty Images
Interior design by Aesthetic Soup

For bulk, special sales, or ministry purchases, please call 1-800-547-8979.
Email: CustomerService@hhpbooks.com

Women of Worth

Published by Harvest House Publishers
Eugene, Oregon 97408
www.harvesthousepublishers.com

ISBN 978-0-7369-9330-2 (pbk)
ISBN 978-0-7369-9331-9 (eBook)

Library of Congress Control Number: 2025937141

Printed in the United States of America

26 27 28 29 30 31 32 33 34 /BP/ 10 9 8 7 6 5 4 3 2 1

"*Women of Worth* is an essential book that offers a much-needed perspective on financial management, written by a woman who understands the unique needs of other women. Whether single, married, wealthy, or poor, women often face common challenges in their financial decisions, driven by fear and confusion due to advertising, peer pressure, and poor advice. This book addresses those issues by providing sound and biblical guidance, helping women become more comfortable and confident in their financial situations. By following God's Word, readers can discover the wisdom and knowledge hidden in Him, leading to a profound yet simple approach to money management.

"Bethany's book is a beautiful combination of both head and heart, offering insights that resonate deeply with women's experiences and effectively communicate the necessary knowledge and perspectives for making informed financial decisions. It highlights the need for every woman to seek to enhance their understanding of money and management. This book is a privilege to endorse and is a must-read for women looking to transform their financial thinking and decision-making."

—**Ron Blue,** founder and ambassador, Ron Blue Institute

"*Women of Worth* is written out of an genuine passion for Christian women to live authentically and generously. In this book, Bethany Frymire shares a very personal journey that encourages each of us to press forward into God's plan and to say *yes* when He calls. You will learn the *why* and the *how* of harnessing the power of money as a tool to confidently fulfill your God-given purpose in your family, your work, your community, and the world."

—**Sharon Epps,** president of Kingdom Advisors
and cofounder of Women Doing Well

"Drawing on nearly 20 years of experience in the financial services industry, Bethany has masterfully interwoven principles of biblical stewardship with practical applications from her personal experience as a financial advisor. I have enjoyed the privilege, as a leader at Blue Trust, of witnessing Bethany's joy in helping single women and couples experience greater confidence and peace of mind in their financial decisions. She shares a powerful message "for such a time as this," as the greatest transfer of wealth in recent history occurs and women are increasingly engaging their hearts and unique talents toward stewarding God's resources to further His kingdom purposes."

—**Brian Shepler,** president/CEO, Blue Trust, Inc.

"Like having a cup of coffee with a friend who happens to be a brilliant financial advisor, this book feels like a conversation that is practical, authentic, and full of real-life wisdom. Bethany invites you into a deeper relationship with God through the unexpected vehicle of money, and somehow makes it feel both natural and profound. This book will put you at ease while challenging you in all the best ways."

—**Julie Wilson,** president, Women Doing Well

To all the women
who have felt less than
or unworthy—

this book is for you.

Contents

Foreword

If you had told me 20 years ago—fresh-faced, working, and only just beginning to learn the rhythm of life as a wife—that I would not return to corporate America and I would, one day, homeschool our kids, write a book, and mentor other women to walk boldly in their God-given calling, I probably would have laughed. Not because I didn't have big dreams of being capable. But because I had been quietly fighting against the influence of culture and certain church traditions to believe that money, leadership, and long-term vision weren't really "my lane."

Now, after 20 years of marriage, seven kids, and countless moments of joy, failure, laughter, and tears, I see things so differently. I've learned, sometimes the hard way, that God never intended for me or any other woman to feel small. We're not called to shrink into the background of our own lives. We are caretakers, stewards, leaders, givers, planners, and visionaries. We've simply too often believed the lies that those titles are not good enough or that they belong to someone else.

That's why *Women of Worth* is such a breath of fresh air—and such a necessary resource. This book doesn't just tell you what to do; it reminds you *who* you are. And sometimes, as women, we need that reminder more than anything else. We need someone to say, "You have what it takes. You're not late. You're not behind. You're right on time, and God is still calling you forward."

Bethany writes not like a distant expert (although she has been doing this work for nearly 20 years), but like a trusted friend. She doesn't throw jargon at you or expect you to have it all figured out before you begin. Instead, she walks with you, chapter by chapter, breaking down finances in a way that's practical, approachable, and infused with God's heart. This book isn't just about money. It's about courage. It's about calling. It's about standing up in your life, however messy or uncertain it may feel, and saying, "Yes, Lord. Use me here. Use me now."

Whether you're single, married, widowed, divorced, working, homeschooling, navigating an empty nest, or feeling like you're still trying to find your footing—this book is for you. It's for the woman who has been playing it small. It's for the woman who is ready to rise but unsure where to start. It's for the woman who has been quietly carrying the weight of her family, her dreams, and her doubts, who just needs a little light to see the next steps.

So here it is. Light for your path. Strength for your heart. Truth for your journey.

You are a woman of worth.

And it's time the world knew it.

Kirsten Watson
Wife of 20 years, mommy to seven, and still learning every day
Author of *Sis, Take a Breath*

Introduction

The You You Long to Be

As Melissa, a dear friend and kingdom-minded financial advisor, slid into the booth across from me, she seemed calm and put together. She was completely at peace and ready to be fully present as we sat down to enjoy tacos and talk finances. As always, she looked elegant, dressed in a professional (and I must add, very cute) dress, blazer, and boots. Guacamole and chips were already on the table, begging to be devoured. Despite the plethora of responsibilities in Melissa's life, she was genuinely attentive whenever we spent time together, unhurried and unguarded. She seemed perfectly confident in who God created her to be. She gently laid her laptop tote down and reached across the table to clasp my hand. The joy and assurance she exuded—simply in knowing who she was in Christ—was palpable. As a colleague in my industry, she was ready to dig into business *and* dive deeper to see how I was really doing, because she truly cared.

Melissa is a life-giver. Now, her life clearly wasn't perfect, but she was living out of who God said she was—she knew her identity, and she walked like she knew.

On the other side of the booth was, well, just plain old me. Hurried.

Questioning. Biting my lip in a constant state of anxiety. Always feeling like it must have been an accident I was invited to a seat in any meeting room. Continually wondering when everyone would realize I was a complete disaster—exposing the fact that I actually had no idea what I was doing—and then deciding I wasn't fit to be the (you name it): mom, Blue Trust employee, wife, friend, or pastor's wife I was thought to be.

"Well, how have you been?" Melissa dipped her first chip into the guacamole.

I floundered inside as I tried to respond with the truth, but not the whole truth. "Oh, I've been great," I said. "You know, always figuring out the juggle. Kids, husband, work, church…and repeat." I picked at the napkin in front of me, wondering how much to share. "It's a joy," I added, "but boy, it's hard. I feel like I can never 'win' in any of these areas. I keep trying and trying, but I never excel in any one role because I'm trying my hardest to do so many things at once." I looked up at her, holding my breath. Could she relate to what I was feeling?

Melissa slowly and thoughtfully nodded as my words soaked in. When she responded, her reply both encouraged and surprised me. "Wow, I feel that," she said. "It was a real learning curve for me to figure out what it looks like to do my best and rest in who Jesus says I am."

Whew! The good news was that I wasn't alone. Melissa admitted she has struggled too. But that learning curve was what had me stuck. How is it possible for some women, like Melissa, to exude peace and confidence, and for others, like me, to take each step unsure if they were worthy to be present?

Reading this book, if you have ever doubted yourself, you are welcome here.

If you've ever wondered why a manager or colleague invited you into an important meeting, then this is the place for you.

If you've ever tried to stay within a budget but failed, hitting the reset button repeatedly just to try again for the millionth time, please have a seat right here next to me.

If you've ever tiptoed into your own bedroom closet with a Reese's peanut butter cup while hiding from your children, please know, I have too.

If you've ever hoped you'd have the energy to make your husband a priority after a long day of giving to everyone else, and yet, once again, you just sat on the couch like a zombie, you are one of my people.

If you've ever thought of investments and financial planning as a "man's world," complicated and enigma-like, rest assured and settle in—you are fully accepted in this space.

If you sincerely and desperately desire to trust God to allow you to make a difference that only you can make in this world, then you, my dear friend, are not alone.

If faith, identity, finances, and professional or at-home roles seem to be a challenge as you doubt your own capability and worth, you have arrived in a place where you can simply take a deep breath.

No, really, let's take a deep breath together.

Imagine a safe place of encouragement and equipping, of fellowship and learning. And imagine that's here. Now. Together. Are you ready for the journey?

You are welcome here. Every part of you! Not just the parts you put on display for others to see. Dig down in your heart and find those parts you usually keep stuffed away—feelings of unworthiness, anxiety, incompetence—yes, those are the parts that are most welcome as we begin our voyage together.

I truly have been—and sometimes still am—the woman across the table who hurried, questioned, doubted my worth and value, and wavered regarding my competency in financial matters and even my ability to understand those matters. You see, I'd been the Friday bagel-bringer in my administrative assistant role at Blue Trust, and I found it unfathomable that God had something else in store.

He had more.

And thankfully, God didn't give up on me. He took me through a most unlikely journey of challenge and encouragement. Heartbreak and redemption. Gentle learning and dependence on Him.

Guess what? God doesn't give up on you either. He quietly waits. He speaks through His Word. He places people in the body of Christ with us at just the right moments to speak life.

To help us to see and believe we are women of worth.

To show us we are fully competent and help us recognize we have the potential to learn, understand, and even become experts in our fields of interest—including financial matters!

To transform us from feeling lost, hurried, and anxious to being confidently known, valued, and loved by the One who matters most.

He has a plan for you. He has a purpose for you. You are not an afterthought, and you never were.

And it's a powerful transformation. There's so much to come. So much hope. If we don't step out to seize what God has for us and step into the unique plan He's crafted for each of us, not only do we miss out, but others miss out as well.

What if it only took a small shift in perspective to see your own worth? What if through the most unlikely of opportunities, you recognized your identity in Jesus, and it flat out changed everything?

Hang with me. Just…what if? What if you are on the verge of a breakthrough—in faith, in finance, or in whatever God has called you to in this season?

Dear friend, God has so much ahead for us—in faith, in finance, and so much more—all so He can reveal the worth He's created in us to change everything for His glory.

1
You Can Thrive

The Power of God Owning It All

Hurricane Katrina.

For me, Katrina creeps up in odd places. Strange times when I haven't thought about her in forever, and then suddenly, she's on me. She finds me when I'm cooking a meal for my family or when I'm driving home on the long commute from the office. She even finds me during the holidays. I'll be surrounded by so much joy, only to be reminded of a time filled with sorrow.

Christmas ornaments are one of my very favorite things. A myriad of memories all in one box. Some heartbreaking, some joyous, and some reminders of mile markers in life. All memories. All part of our family's journey. Carefully pulling them out of the box each year is a joy. My husband Landon's task is to haul the extremely large, nine-foot Costco artificial Christmas tree down from the attic and piece it together in the corner of our living room. Then, our two boys, James and Silas, and I make it our mission to decorate the tree together. I relish every single ornament that comes out of the box.

In early January one year, as I pulled each ornament off the tree to pack it away for the next Christmas, I paused to hold one of my most special ornaments gingerly in my palm. I lingered as I rolled it around in my hand and thought about how precious this particular ornament is to me. Not because it's a Precious Moments ornament, though as a child of the '80s, I do love some Precious Moments pieces. But instead, because of what it symbolizes—survival through Hurricane Katrina and the reminder that God owns it all.

Hurricane Katrina sweeping through our home in 2005 is seared in my memory. We'd owned our home for three months, and then *bam*, the hurricane arrived when Landon had only just attended his first two weeks of seminary. At the time, seminary in Louisiana was to be a whole new journey…or so we thought. God had paved the way. He moved swiftly, surely, and incredibly to show us He wanted us to move to New Orleans. So, of course, after Katrina, all of this left us asking one question: Why?

God began to reveal His plan two years before Katrina hit. We were in our Crestview, Florida, bathroom as Landon and I brushed our teeth before bed one late Wednesday evening. Only three months into our marriage, I'd just witnessed my brand-new husband share Jesus with the youth of our church that night. And I was floored. Landon's degree was in surveying and engineering from the University of Florida. And he was surveying. You know, doing the thing he received a degree to do. His career path looked solid. That is, until that Wednesday evening.

Our trajectory seemed much less certain after that. I'll never forget standing in our 1990s hunter-green Formica countertop bathroom with a pink toothbrush hanging out of my mouth when Landon blurted out, "I think I'm called to preach. I think I'm supposed to be in ministry."

Whoa now. Let's take a minute and get the toothbrushes out of our mouths and just think about what he was saying here.

And we did. We thought and prayed about it and sought counsel from wise men and women around us. And God made it clear that New Orleans Baptist Theological Seminary was the path He had ahead for Landon and me.

It was May 2005 when we pushed the "go" button. God worked literal miracles that seemed impossible. He set up an ideal living situation for us in Slidell, Louisiana, a town right outside of New Orleans. We bought a home—with no mortgage, mind you, which only God could have orchestrated. And we pulled out of Crestview in a U-Haul moving truck, headed west on Interstate 10 to a new chapter: seminary.

I began work as a bank teller and Landon readied himself to begin his master of divinity studies in the fall. We started to settle in, until the end of August, when the weather forecast showed a hurricane was headed our way.

As a brand-new employee of the bank, on the Friday before the hurricane hit, I asked my supervisor, "I see this hurricane looks like it's moving in our direction. What should I do if I can't make it to work on Monday morning?" My supervisor didn't know me from a stranger down the street yet, and it seemed she thought I was trying to get out of work. I'll never forget her disdainful look when she said, "That hurricane is not going to hit here. You need to plan to be here Monday morning."

As we continued to follow the probable track of the storm, we prepared as best we could—boarding up windows (as we had done in Florida with hurricanes we'd become used to all our lives) and gathering important documents. Then we headed home, back to the panhandle of Florida, to watch the news and wait for the storm to blow through.

And blow through it did. Early Monday morning, as we sat in my parents' living room and watched The Weather Channel, our Slidell ADT alarm notified us that our back door had been breached. At the time, we weren't sure what that meant. Wind? Rain? Flooding?

We soon found out. In the early days after the storm, we knew nothing. No one knew anything. We found an AM radio station with reports of what homeowners were finding as they attempted to return to their properties. And just shy of a week after the storm, Landon and I returned—with both of our dads joining us for the day trip—in my dad's Chevrolet truck, carrying our own gas to ensure we could safely return to the panhandle that evening.

As we crossed from Alabama into Mississippi on I-10, the most horrid odor I've ever smelled—to this day—entered the truck. I still not so fondly refer to this smell as "Slidell mud." The stench of the hurricane. Of the flooding. Of the destruction and loss. And the mold. Mainly, the mold.

We dodged downed power lines and various dangers to finally, thankfully, pull into our Slidell driveway. The scene was absolutely apocalyptic and still seems surreal to even think about.

Our home was a total loss. It was still standing. And the water had receded. But we could see the water line had reached around five feet high. Mud was everywhere—mud on the floor, mud on the furniture, a thin coating of mud throughout everything. The refrigerator toppled over. Dressers lay sideways on the floor with drawers broken and clothes spilling out. The roof in our bedroom closet caved in, opening straight up to the blue and sunny sky, ruining every piece of clothing we owned.

And we began to question.

Only months earlier, we'd had no doubt. Absolutely no doubt.

Not one iota.

But then, three months later, after God paved the way, our new chapter was wiped out by Katrina? Why?

Left with muddy and moldy everything and sobbing in my parents' driveway while I exhaustedly hosed off fine china, dark nights followed. I was bleaching Christmas ornaments in the kitchen sink. We tried our hardest to save special moments and memories. Yearbooks, letterman jackets, an entire library given to Landon by a spiritual mentor, all my beloved piano books and more—gone. All our worldly belongings fit into less than ten boxes in my parents' foyer, and the rest of our worldly goods were piled out by the road of our shell of a house in a moldy, wet, smelly mountain. And it looked like all might be lost. It looked confusing. It looked like we had zigged when God told us to zag. But did we?

Absolutely not.

Because, in the next few months, the Father clearly (just as clearly as He sent us to New Orleans) paved a new road. An unimaginably beautiful road for us to move to Woodstock, Georgia. For me to find a career with the firm I'm still with today, nearly 20 years later. He orchestrated a plan for Landon to attend an extension of his New Orleans seminary in Atlanta, and He provided an incredible opportunity for Landon to mentor with our new pastor in Woodstock. We could have given up. We could have said, "Just forget it," and stayed in Florida. Landon could have gone back to work as a surveyor and we could have settled back into our old life.

Staring at the bleached-out Precious Moments Christmas ornament in my hand reminded me, once again, that God owns it all. He doesn't just own what I think I've "allowed" Him to own. God is sovereign and, as His children, just as Proverbs 16:9 tells us, He directs our steps. At the very moment that all looks lost, it's actually beginning. It's a new fire kindling, the start of new life. I learned then, and I've continued to learn over these past twenty-or-so years, that when God allows death in my life, it brings forth more life than I could have imagined.

As I began to learn and embrace the knowledge that God owns it all, through Katrina, I began to see that money and worldly goods were not everything they were cracked up to be. The trappings of this world are fun and comfortable, and they feel like a necessity until God allows them to be stripped away. And He began to teach me what it truly meant for me to believe that He does own it all.

What Money Is

So what does that lesson tell us? Understanding God owns it all means I have developed a healthy, biblical view surrounding money. What money is and, as equally important, what it isn't.

As I often share with my Blue Trust clients: Money is a tool; money is a test; and money can be a testimony.

Money Is Neutral—It Is Simply a Tool

Philippians 4:11-13 says, "I am not saying this because I am in need, for I have learned to be content whatever the circumstances. I know what it is to be in need, and I know what it is to have plenty. I have learned the secret of being content in any and every situation, whether well fed or hungry, whether living in plenty or in want. I can do all this through him who gives me strength."

I wish I could say I've easily embraced what Paul shares here—living contentedly whether overflowing with worldly possessions or looking in the rearview mirror at my Slidell home with all my belongings covered in black mold and sitting by the road in a messy pile. But I'm a work in progress, and as God continues to gently remind me, I can be content in Him. He's the one who provides. He's the one who has the plan. He's the one who will wisely show me how to handle this tool.

Money Is a Test

Luke 16:13 says, "No one can serve two masters. Either you will hate the one and love the other, or you will be devoted to the one and despise the other. You cannot serve both God and money."

I know most of us have experienced this testing—this pull—because the world tells us that more is good. More is the right way. Just get more, and you'll be secure and satisfied. You have a thousand dollars? You'd better get two thousand. You have two thousand? You'd better get three. You have ten thousand? You'd better get twenty thousand. And why? The world whispers the lie, "Build bigger barns. So you'll be worth something. Build those barns. Don't consider the eternal. The right now is all there is."

Money Can Be a Testimony

If you pull up the Frymire family's credit union checking account, you can see what our priorities are (and a good bit of eating out between sports practices). I can talk a lot about giving and generosity, and those may be my intentions, but my true actions—the choices I'm making—are laid bare if you type in that username and password and look at my bank transactions. I don't say that as a judgment. Or an indictment. I say it as a first step. We must evaluate ourselves and ask the Holy Spirit to show us. Show us how our lives can be a testimony of God's love and faithfulness through our time, our talents, and our treasure. Are we going to place our hope in the uncertainty of riches? Do we look any different from the world?

What Money Is Not

Just as money is a tool, a test, and can be a testimony, something else I often share with my financial planning clients is that money is *not* a measure of self-worth, a guarantee of contentment, a reward for godly living, or a measure of success.

Money Is Not a Measure of Self-Worth

A lie of the world is, "You're only worth something if you drive a nice car, if you don't wear the same work outfit twice in one week, or if you have the top-of-the-line (fill in the blank)." The world tells us, "Everyone is watching you. They will all notice. They'll think you're nothing if you don't buy the bigger home, carry the designer bag, or purchase the platinum edition of your vehicle instead of the plain-old basic model."

Ephesians 2:10 says, "For we are His workmanship, created in

Christ Jesus for good works, which God prepared beforehand, that we should walk in them" (ESV).

Dear friend, I know you want to walk in those good works just like I do. As Jesus followers, our heart's desire—because this is how He's created us—is to pursue Him, to pursue eternal things, and to pursue the things that really matter. But the gosh darn world just gets in the way. The last thing I want to happen—and I desperately mean this—is to reach the end of my life and realize that God prepared good works for me, and I chose not to walk in them. I chose not to walk in them because I believed lies. I was sucked into the mirage that my whole identity—who I am—is tied up in what I do or do not own.

Deuteronomy 8:17-18 says, "Otherwise, you may say in your heart, 'My power and the strength of my hand made me this wealth.' But you shall remember the LORD your God, for it is He who is giving you the power to make wealth" (NASB). Interestingly, the Bible never says it's a sin to have wealth. The problem is that when we do have wealth, it's insanely difficult *not* to get our identity tied up in that wealth. And there's the rub.

No matter the size of our wealth, we always want to be asking God, "What would You have me do with *Your* wealth today? How can I grow *Your* kingdom today and not my own?" Our prayer should be, "Lord, show me what lasts for eternity, and give me wisdom to see through the lie that my self-worth is derived from my net worth."

Money Isn't a Guarantee of Contentment

There has been—and continues to be—instance after instance in my own life where I've saved up for something. Maybe I saved for months. Maybe for years. And then I got what I was saving for. *Yes*, I finally got it! What happened next? You guessed it. The very next day I think of something else that I don't have. Solomon speaks directly to this cycle in Ecclesiastes 1:8, "All things are wearisome;

no one can tell it. The eye is not satisfied with seeing, nor is the ear filled with hearing" (NASB). Wow, what an "encouragement" (I hope you sense my sarcasm). *So I'm never going to be satisfied while on this earth? I'm going to feel a constant tension between the next thing I'm convinced will bring me contentment versus feeling content with what I already have?* Yes.

I have a dear friend who has battled this for years. On the surface, she is calm and appears confident and content in her life choices. But underneath, she flounders in finding her identity in Christ, believing money will finally bring her contentment. I can almost see her breathe a sigh of relief as she builds yet another home, time after time.

From a modest home to a vastly larger home with delightful builder upgrades. That was surely it. This was going to solve all her problems. Family dysfunction would be *poof*—gone. Marital strife would be healed if she and her husband just had that special coffee bar and a fireplace in their bedroom. Two dishwashers would clearly make life easier—one always clean and one always dirty. And space for the kids to spread out. And at first, after closing on the larger home, it felt good. My friend seemed settled and calmer. But within the first few months, it was clear that she was back to her old, discontented thoughts, ways, and attitudes of the heart.

Suddenly, the house was simply too big. It was too big to allow for family time. There was too much room to spread out. The house was too big to clean. It was too expensive to hire a housekeeper. You get my drift. This precious sister in Christ then moved in the opposite direction. In the next couple of years, her family sold the larger house and moved into a drastically smaller home. Siblings were sharing rooms and bathrooms. There was a tiny living room with everyone crammed together for quality time. But still, the same theme remained. Discontent.

You can probably identify with my friend, and so can I. Numerous times a day I have thoughts like, *Man, I want a new couch. Our kids have destroyed our couch, and I really want a new one. It would make me so happy to have a new couch.* Or, *If only I could afford a Peloton. I really would be in shape if I just had a Peloton—I'd bet it would change everything. I just know I'd want to work out then.*

Your thoughts may not center on a new couch or a Peloton, but there is something. We are all human, and this is a battle we all fight. Do you hear Jesus whispering over us? "Dear One," He says, "Rest in Me. Take a breath. Stop paddling under the surface where no one else knows you're struggling. I am the one who brings contentment." I know you desire, as I do, to simply rest. It takes daily—sometimes moment by moment—communication with the Holy Spirit to remind us of who we are. And whose we are. And where our value, identity, and worth all lie.

Money Is Not a Reward for Godly Living

When Landon was on the surveying track for his career, I was pumped. Early on in our marriage, I envisioned his career track—maybe owning his own surveying company one day—really digging in and pursuing the next career goal and the next after that. Like duh, we all know that if you check off the boxes and live a godly life, God will reward you. *Right?*

Did you check off boxes on your offering envelope when you were a child? I sure did. I attended a Southern Baptist church—First Baptist Church of DeFuniak Springs—and let me tell you, I received a box of offering envelopes each quarter that had my very own name on them. One envelope per week. I would walk into Sunday school with my offering envelope in hand. There were literally checkboxes printed on the envelope to mark off, and someone was tracking them. Items like, "Read my Bible each day," "Studied my Sunday school lesson," and so on.

Now, there were many, many wonderful things about the years

growing up in my church and becoming a Christian at eight years old. That beloved environment helped to build my foundation in trusting Jesus with my life, for *all* my life. But I will tell you, checking off those boxes really helped play into the lie that if I could just check off the boxes in life, my life would go well. It would be fairly easy, and I would be rewarded with, well, rewards, and one of those rewards would obviously be money.

But then, Landon and I started down the ministry track. And goodness knows that no one goes into ministry for the money. While there were times I've been unsure how God would provide throughout the ministry journey we've been on, He has always been faithful, and we have never, ever lacked for anything we needed. As we've made ministry transitions and faithfully served the people God called us to serve during each assignment, it has become clearer and clearer that there are no checkboxes. No one is waiting to take my offering envelope where I've checked off all the things I did "right" during the week. Life can be hard. Like, *really* hard. Even when you are living a godly life and closely walking with the Lord day by day. Those new mercies? Good grief, I need them.

Money Is Not a Measure of Success

We live in northeast Georgia and drive home to the panhandle of Florida several times each year to visit our families. I know this drive like the back of my hand, as we've been making it now for nearly 20 years. And, I love to ride in the car. My very favorite thing to do—as a reward—when work is stressful or life just gets to be too much, is to ask Landon to drive me around to look at houses on country roads while I sip my venti hot white mocha from Starbucks. And maybe enjoy a birthday cake pop.

As Landon drives us home for family visits, many times I look out the window as we pass through towns and neighborhoods. We stay on the interstates through Atlanta, but once we get south of Atlanta, there's an exit near the Kia plant with a huge flyover. Silas, my ten-year-old, loves the flyover because it makes him feel like we're on a racetrack.

Once we leave the interstate, we are immersed in small-town life for the remainder of the six-hour journey. Different small towns. One after the other. All the same, yet all a little different. But there's usually something each town has in common. I wonder if you have noticed it where you live? In the towns on our drive, normally, there's a great big house on the outskirts. Maybe it is owned by a lawyer, or a banker, or just a guy or girl with a lot of money. Then, after leaving that town, you come to the next town. There's a McDonald's, maybe a Chick-fil-A if the town is fancy, and then the outskirts and that same (but slightly different) great big house. The great big house where this particular town's lawyer, banker, or person with a lot of money lives. And there's nothing wrong with living in a big house. We've already established that money is a tool—it's not good or bad. But it's wise to recognize the same pattern. The same thing over and over and over. It's called the principle of limited sphere.

Likely, the big-house person in the first town doesn't know the big-house person in the second town, and those two big-house people don't know the big-house person in the third town, and so on. If I make it my ambition and heart's desire to amass as much money as I can, as many worldly goods as I can, so what? How many people am I actually going to impact? Maybe 200 people? We all live in a limited sphere. It's because of this principle that we absolutely cannot allow ourselves, as Christians, to believe the lie that money makes us successful. I pray the Lord will open my eyes to see what is eternal—what does *not* have a limited sphere—and allow me to join Him where He's working.

Success in this life is a function of being obedient to what God has called each of us to. It has nothing to do with a monetary measurement. A verse that is familiar to many, Psalm 139:14, says, "I will praise you, for I am fearfully and wonderfully made" (NKJV). And Jeremiah 29:11 teaches us that God has a plan for each of us—to prosper us and not harm us, to give us hope and a future. Also, Romans 8:28 reminds us that God is working all things for our good and His glory. As we digest what money is and isn't, and as we attempt to allow those truths to soak in and reveal *the* truth to us, I pray you will remember and know beyond a shadow of a doubt: God has a plan for *you*.

When you seek to understand, remember, and live out the truth that God owns it all, you can live securely. With or without great wealth. With or without a pool. With or without a coffee bar. And, for me, with or without that Peloton bike. God has called each of us to something great. Vital to our identity is building a strong and biblical foundation for what money is and what it is not. This foundation gives us the confidence to take the next steps as we walk in His plans for us.

My precious Christmas ornament still smells like Slidell mud. And it is a gross, grayed-out color from soaking it in dish soap and bleach water. It holds the marks of what it's been through. And so do I. I wear the imprints of this life—all the joy, all the pain, and all the hard things. God is weaving the tapestry of my life beyond what I know and can see. And I'm counting on it. Because sometimes, the hard stuff in this world doesn't make sense. I can't understand it. *And it just keeps coming*. And I try. Oh, I try. I pull up my bootstraps and keep pushing forward, committing to just try harder, again and again and again. That's my jam—just trying harder. But my ornament. It reminds me that I'm not in control. God owns it all. I need to let go. There's a plan, and I'm not the leader. He brings beauty from ashes, life from death, and beautiful Christmas ornaments from Slidell mud.

2

Your Heart in Action

Beginning with God's End in Mind

Several years back, when I stepped into my boss's office for my annual review, I could not have fathomed I would walk out a different person. No one else immediately noticed, but inside, the Holy Spirit lit a spark that would turn into a flame and change everything.

Most of us who work in a corporate job look forward to an annual review like we look forward to a dentist appointment. Especially the kind of dentist appointment where you take the awkward bitewing x-rays. The whole time, you're gagging and choking while trying to swallow your own spit but attempting to keep your cool. For me, dreading my annual reviews never reached a level that extreme, but I certainly never counted down the days to each one with excitement.

This particular year, as I stepped into the office of Jeff Chinery, the managing director of our Everyday Steward division at Blue Trust, I didn't feel dread or great anticipation. Jeff's workspace was always inviting, but not because of the room's neutral decor or the large windows that let in sunlight. His smile was genuine and his Bible was open on his desk as he welcomed me in and motioned for me to sit down. I was prepared for a status-quo conversation. I anticipated the conversation would consist of comments like:

"Bethany, you're doing a great job in your role."

"How's it going balancing work and your family?"

"What do you plan to work on this next year to improve in your role?"

I'm sure our conversation *did* include that comment and those questions. But it also included more. A switch was flipped in my life that day.

Up until that point, my work at Blue Trust had been fulfilling, and I was fully content in my various roles. From beginning as an administrative assistant, then moving to Human Resources, and finally stepping in to our firm's Everyday Steward division several years later. It was as if God was, unbeknownst to me, building a foundation—one brick at a time—and placing a variety of tools in my toolbelt. I was completely oblivious to His plan, but God knew. The Father knew He had good plans for me, and He opened one door after the other at just the right moments.

I always assumed I would serve in a support role. While working full-time before children and working part-time while my boys were babies, I supported others through my work. Though there was never an overt, audible message, my subconscious screamed out: "You are made for a support role. Your purpose is only to support others on their journeys."

Do you see the opposite message? What I really was telling myself was this: *You are not a leader. No one wants to support you. God doesn't have a journey for you. God's journey for you is to help others with the special journeys He has for them.*

Eye opening, right?

And support others, I did. At work. At home, as a wife and a mom. At church, as a pastor's family. Support, support, and more support. And heaven knows, there's nothing wrong with a support role. Support roles are amazing *if* that is what God is calling us to. But let's be clear: What God is not calling us to do is to place ourselves in a comfortable box and sit crisscross applesauce without even asking Him what He may have for us in His plans.

As Jeff began to walk through this memorable annual review with me, suddenly, the conversation took an unexpected turn.

"Do you have a dream here?" Jeff asked, as he leaned forward with genuine interest and care. "I believe you could do anything you want to do."

Hard stop. I stared at him like he had 20 heads. I was happy with what I was doing. I was settled. I was content. I was supporting people and the business.

But his words pierced a new place in my heart I didn't even know existed. His words soaked deep into my soul, in a place where the Holy Spirit whispered, "My precious daughter, I have more for you."

And for a reason I could not understand at the time, tears began to well up in my eyes. I was shocked to hear the words he had spoken.

"Me?" I said. My jaw dropped as my mind began to immediately swirl with questions and disbelief. "You think I could do anything I want to do here?"

And in his usual, unhurried, and calming way, he nodded reassuringly.

"Yes," Jeff said, as if I'd just asked him the simplest question in the world. He shrugged and looked me straight in the face. "There's no question in my mind. Let's figure it out together."

And that was when the switch flipped. A switch I didn't even realize was turned off. That switch turned on a light in my life and my work and gave me purpose in a way I'd never experienced before. It invited me on an unanticipated, difficult, and wildly fulfilling journey.

Where before, I had been asking, "Who can I support and how?" my question shifted to, "What kind of kingdom impact could I have here?"

As Jesus followers, each of us should be asking this question. We're all making an impact—whether we recognize it or not. And our impact does not only come through our support roles or our leadership roles (where I learned this lesson), or through our other roles in different arenas of life. It also comes through looking at how we steward our finances. Let's take a deeper look.

Stewarding Our Finances—Making Money a Nonissue

Raise your hand if you'd like to spend more time focusing on your own personal finances. My hand is not raised and is stiffly glued to my side. As I seek to fulfill God's calling and have kingdom impact in each area of my life, I recognize that finances are a piece of the puzzle I must be willing to wrap my mind around. It is vital that I understand my financial situation and feel confident in the decisions I make, so that I can focus on the areas of life that really matter; thereby making finances a nonissue. But practically, how in the world is it possible to make finances a nonissue?

For me, this thought seems laughable and ridiculously impossible. Amid the tasks of continual laundry where people leave their clothes inside out, making dinners that only half my family likes, delivering financial plans and helping clients make investment decisions, and carting my children around like I'm a taxi driver...sure, no problem. I have plenty of time to get a handle on my finances—*not.*

The good news is that making finances a nonissue *is* possible. Thankfully, there are practical tips and tools that can help us move to a place of peace in our finances so that we can truly focus on what matters most.

Carve Out Time for Annual Goal Planning

If you're married, have you ever done any intentional goal planning with your spouse? And if you're not married, have you ever set aside time to think about your goals as an individual? Either way, whatever season of life you're in, intentionality when it comes to creating goals for yourself and your family is vital to achieving those goals.

As a full-time financial advisor and working mom and wife, I have many good intentions. Sometimes I have great ideas. Impactful ideas. Thoughts and impressions I feel the Father has placed on my heart. But without some kind of intentionality to help me capture these ideas and execute them, many times I'm simply surviving life in the best way with time passing by quickly. Then I realize the dreams and goals God may have given me aren't happening because I haven't taken intentional time to make a plan.

Proverbs 16:9 says, "The heart of man plans his way, but the Lord establishes his steps" (ESV).

For the Lord to direct our steps, we must give Him focused time when we listen to what He may be impressing upon our hearts. This is not something that happens by chance at ten o'clock at night when I'm exhausted. If my husband and I have important conversations at that late hour, the conversations usually don't end with powerful spiritual insights. They end in exhaustion and sometimes disharmony. Always, my desire is for my words to be shared with gracious speech (Colossians 4:6) as I partner with Landon for God's glory.

I encourage you to set aside a window of time each year for annual goal planning, whether you are married or single. A time you step out of your regular routine of life and pray, spending time alone with God to ask and listen as He guides you regarding what He may want you to do or accomplish in the future. As He speaks and guides, you want to record your goals so they are clearly defined and measurable. Doing this is never convenient, but it's always—*always*—worth it.

And don't forget: Goals are based on faith and following God's leading, not on past accomplishments or current resources. Ephesians 3:20 tells us that God can do "abundantly far more than all we can ask or imagine" (NRSV). If God has given you a God-sized dream, trust Him in it! Remember, if God calls us, He'll equip us!

Find a Budgeting Method that Works for You

When considering your budget, let's start with this question: Are you purposefully giving, saving, and spending? Before jumping into a budgeting system, let's briefly address what we can actually do with our money. Where can our income go?

At Blue Trust, we believe there are five ways we use money:

- Charitable giving
- Paying taxes

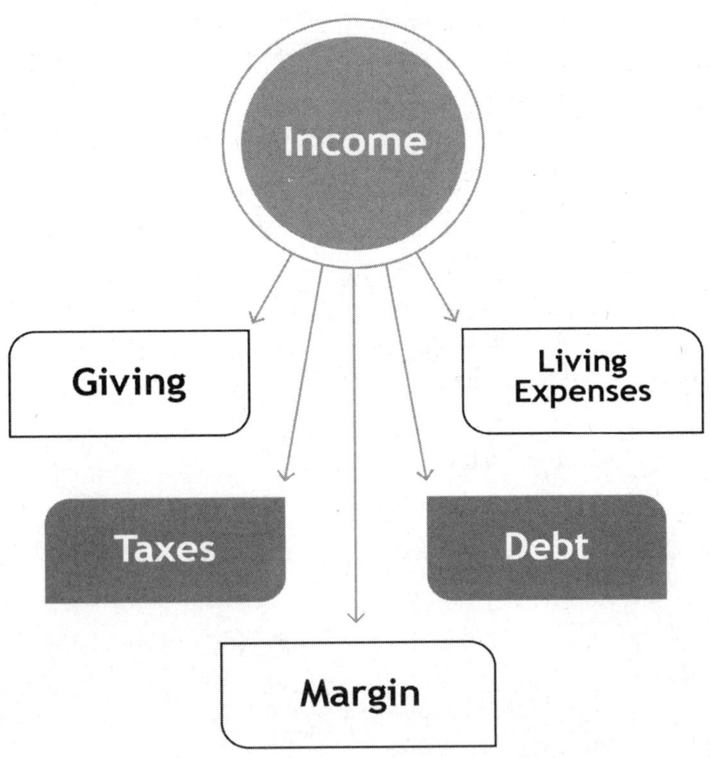

- Paying off debt
- Living expenses (like groceries, housing, utility bills, gas for your car)
- Margin (save, spend, or invest)

What's left over after the first four uses is what we call *margin*. We can spend our margin, or we can save or invest it. If you have margin, it means you are spending less than you earn, which is the key to accomplishing your future financial goals!

So how do you succeed and gain clarity when organizing these five uses?

I know you're probably thinking, *Budget. This is a budget. Bethany is saying we must have a budget.* Well, maybe, but hang with me, there's more to it. Living on some type of budget brings freedom because you know where your boundaries and parameters are. It relieves stress and anxiety. But we're all wired differently, and different budgeting methods speak to each of us in various ways. Ranging from a supersized spreadsheet that tracks every single transaction of your life all the way down to a more general bucketing system. Think through how God has made you, and lean into your personality to find a budgeting tool that is helpful to you. The worst thing you could do is try to implement a system that is unsustainable and complicated if what you're doing now is working. But we do know it's vital to be purposeful in how we steward the resources God has given us.

Bucket Budgeting

For anyone like me who loves to set up a budget but doesn't actually have time to keep up with that budget, I'd like to introduce a concept called bucket budgeting.

Basically, bucket budgeting is a bit like setting up a traditional budget, but the greatest thing about it is that once you do the work of setting it up—with the exception of every once in a while if you need to make adjustments—it works on its own without much thought or maintenance. The end goal of utilizing this type of spending plan is clarity and simplicity. You spend little time managing the process and you have freedom in discretionary spending because you know how much is available.

Here's the basic concept:

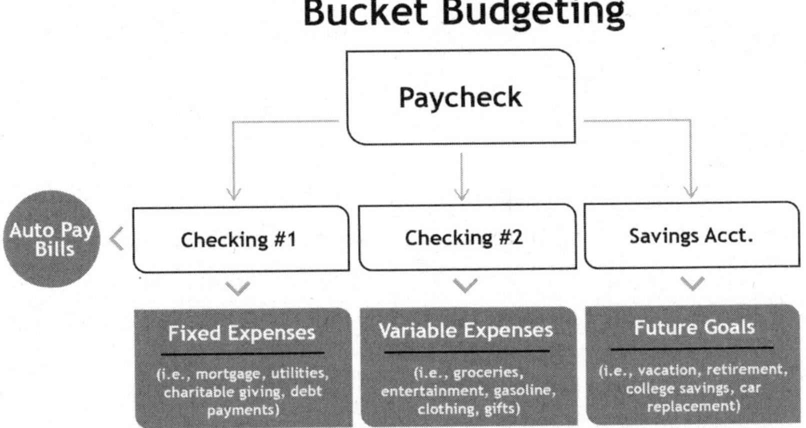

You will set up:

- Two checking accounts:
    - Checking account #1 for fixed expenses
    - Checking account #2 for variable expenses
- A savings account that gives you the ability to create buckets/savings goals within it to prioritize and provide clarity

Checking account #1 will be for your fixed expenses. This is what we can refer to as your "bills" account. Your charitable giving, debt payments, utility bills, gas for your car—anything that is generally the same each month or in the ballpark of the same amount will come from this account. You'll want to figure out what that dollar amount is, and direct that amount into your fixed expenses checking account each month. I recommend setting up automatic payments (auto pay) for as many of these expenses as possible, just to simplify! Also keep in mind that some companies and organizations will provide a discount or small financial perk if you set up auto pay. Initially, fund this account with a good cushion (maybe a month or so extra of these fixed expenses) to ensure that you have plenty to start with if an electric or water bill comes in higher than you anticipate once in a while.

Let's skip checking account #2 for a moment and talk through the savings account.

You'll want to set up a savings account, and ideally, a savings account that allows you to create different buckets you can name and direct funds toward. There are several online savings accounts that allow you to do this, and this approach gives clarity and freedom in saving for certain goals and then feeling the freedom to spend within those buckets. For instance, my savings buckets look like this:

- Insurance paid annually or biannually—to prepare and anticipate those recurring costs that don't happen monthly
- New car fund—where I'm paying myself a car payment before my next vehicle purchase
- Vacation bucket—to save up for relaxing trips
- School expenses—camps, extracurricular activities, sports fees, etc. for my sons

My kids are in a season of life in which they are playing sports and doing all kinds of school activities that add up financially and are expensive. When I create a "school activities" bucket and steadily fund it over time, the money is there when my family needs it. You can fund these buckets per paycheck or periodically—whatever works for you.

Now, back to checking account #2. This checking account will be used for what's called your variable expenses. You're already depositing money into the main checking account for bills and fixed expenses. Also, you're sending money to steadily build your savings buckets. Whatever is left over can go into this second checking account for periodic or variable expenses. This account helps me and my family answer a lot of spending questions. Can we eat out after church on Sunday? Can I send flowers to my son's teacher to encourage her? Could I meet friends and see a movie this week? I'm not stealing from the bills account to do "extra" things, and I'm not spending funds that I should be saving. I have a true understanding regarding how much "extra" I have.

For many, the bucket budgeting approach has brought great clarity and insight into their finances. And, keep in mind, if you are married, it's crucial for both spouses to work through this bucket budgeting process together. If I work on it alone, I'll miss areas Landon finds important, or I'll set an unrealistic budget limit for a category I have nothing to do with (like yard work!). If Landon works on this process without me, he'll have no idea what a realistic vacation savings goal would be and would not know how much money in total we spend on gas as I commute back and forth to work each month. When married, we must be willing to engage with our spouse as an active, willing, and equal partner—as a woman of worth!—in any and all financial discussions.

Budgeting Brings Peace of Mind

The world generally defines "success" in terms of income and lifestyle, but in God's eyes, these things are unimportant. How we spend our money speaks volumes about our priorities and our belief systems. If we believe that God truly owns it all, every spending decision is, in reality, a spiritual decision.

I was reminded of this truth on an ordinary Wednesday afternoon a few years back. My chocolate chip protein bar wrapper crinkled in my hand as I swung around in my desk chair, tossing my garbage into the trash can. The day was proving to be a Zoom meeting marathon, and I was enjoying my only 30-minute reprieve between calls. With my mind full of to-dos from the day's completed Zoom calls, and thoughts of preparation for the meetings to come, I thoughtfully—but hurriedly—chewed my protein bar. Holding the bar in my left hand, I tapped my keyboard to enter notes with my chocolate-free right hand.

Unexpectedly, my office phone rang. I sighed. To answer or not to answer? That was the question. On the one hand, my next Zoom was fast approaching. On the other hand, if I didn't handle whatever this was now, I'd be handling it later. I swallowed my current bite of chocolate chip goodness and took the call.

"Hello, this is Bethany with Blue Trust."

"Hi, Bethany, this is Sue Childers."

I smiled. Sue and her husband, Steve, were some of my financial planning clients. I'd completed their plan about three months before, so I wasn't expecting to hear from Sue.

"Sue, what a great surprise!" I set what remained of my bar on my desk and leaned back in my chair. "How are you and Steve?"

"We're fantastic, Bethany, and I just had to call and share the best news with you." I could hear her joy through the phone, so I hurriedly flipped open my leather portfolio and clicked on my pen to take notes. Whatever "best news" Sue was preparing to share sounded important. I glanced at the clock—ten minutes until my next call. Still, I turned my attention back to Sue to ensure I was fully present. She was clearly excited, and I wanted to celebrate the moment with her.

"You won't believe it, Bethany!" Sue said. "We just had the best vacation we've ever taken in our entire marriage."

"That's wonderful, Sue!" I was happy for her, yet the mystery remained—what did this have to do with me?

"But, Bethany, I have to tell you why it was the best." Though it was a phone call, I could imagine her beaming from the other end of the line. "Remember during our financial planning time together how we talked about bucket budgeting?"

I nodded, chuckling a little to myself because she could not see me, and continued to listen.

"Remember how we talked about setting up the savings buckets so we could visually see the different goals we were saving for?"

"Absolutely, Sue," I said as I nodded again, keeping my eyes on my notes and ignoring the clock. "I sure do remember that. I recall you sharing that each time you took a vacation—even though you specifically saved for the time away—it still felt like you were stealing from the money you needed for other savings goals." The conversation came back to me as if we'd had it yesterday. "With all your savings grouped together in one pile, you said it was difficult to separate the funds in your mind to enjoy the vacation time."

"Yes, exactly!" Sue confirmed. "That's how I felt. Every time we would eat out on vacation, I worried the whole time as we all ordered expensive meals. Then when the check came, I felt sick thinking of how much we'd spent, all the while knowing we'd saved for the vacation and had the money for it. Still, deep inside, I felt extremely stressed and in emotional turmoil."

I could sense the best part of the story was yet to come, so I waited in anticipation.

"We just returned from vacation yesterday, and you are my first call," Sue continued. "I had to tell you how much the savings buckets helped me mentally, allowing me to enjoy our time away. After our meeting a few months ago, we did just as you recommended. We chose an online bank that would allow us to create various savings goals, and we separated our savings balance into those different goals. I had so much more peace of mind on vacation."

The peace she expressed was tangible, radiating through the line.

"Steve even commented on how relaxed I seemed as we spent the money we'd planned for—eating out together, enjoying excursions, and blessing our children and grandbabies. Handling our savings this way allowed me to breathe a deep sigh of relief, and I just wanted to thank you. Learning how to utilize savings buckets to separate different savings goals was one of the most impactful takeaways from our work with you."

The smile on my face, alone in my office, was enormous. All I could think about was how making financial matters a nonissue helps us focus on what *really* matters. Steve and Sue proved this truth in real life as they vacationed together and enjoyed their time away. How rewarding! As I finished my bar, took a drink of water, and swung around toward my desk to click into my next Zoom call, my heart soared. One individual at a time. One family at a time. Impacting lives for the kingdom.

Plan for the Unexpected

Unfortunately, throughout my time as a financial advisor, I've seen other families experience heartbreak. I've sat across the table from many new widows and widowers. I've cried tears with these precious spouses who never anticipated their wife or husband being taken from this earth earlier than they anticipated. Most would say, "We talked about life insurance and having a will drafted. But we were just so busy. I kept thinking we'd have plenty of time in the future before something happened to one of us."

Planning for the unexpected can be a not-so-fun topic, but it is vital to ensure your loved ones will be prepared when something happens to you. It's simply too important not to ask about and plan for.

Insurance can protect and provide for you and your loved ones. Buying insurance does not signal a lack of faith, but demonstrates prudence and good stewardship in planning for an uncertain future. In most situations, a level term life insurance policy (meaning a defined number of years at a cost that remains the same) is sufficient for your needs, and a good rule of thumb is to have between ten and 15 times your income as a life insurance death benefit. Always look forward to a time when you may be what the financial industry refers to as "self-insured"—when your savings and investment balances outweigh the balances of your liabilities. But also consider your goals personally. Do you wish to leave an inheritance to your children? To a charity? To extended family?

Also, it's crucial to walk through an estate planning process. This process looks different depending on each individual's personal situation, but generally, every person needs a will and related documents that include a durable power of attorney and an advance healthcare directive. When a loved one passes away, I pray it will be a time to grieve, not panic about where paperwork is and how to find what you need to work through a process that may already feel foreign and completely overwhelming. Remember, how you leave your estate will have a significant impact on your heirs. An estate plan can communicate who you are and what's important to you. So we're not just talking about passing along money—we're talking about passing along character, values, and a legacy.

Manage the Juggle of Work-Life Balance

Goal planning, finding a budgeting system that actually works, and experiencing the peace of knowing we have life insurance and estate documents helps to build a solid foundation so that we truly can focus on what's most important.

Laid on top of all we've covered is the serious matter of *time*. Being pulled in a million directions. Trust me, I know the juggle and the struggle are both very real. Being a full-time working wife and mom is not easy, but I have no doubt it is exactly what God has called me to.

Many of us will spend our lives chasing the dream of work-life balance. Even with the best of intentions, the balance will never be perfect, and there will always be seasons where we're leaning into one or the other. In fact, I often need to remind myself that my best is good enough, because as women, we are extremely hard on ourselves. While I nearly kill myself to keep all the plates spinning, it always feels like one is falling. Some piece of my juggling act is dropping, and that's usually the piece I choose to direct my focus toward. The area nearing failure, not the other areas where I am succeeding. The truth is that women who desire to be fully present in the work God has called them to *and* fully present in whatever personal role or season of life they are in are incredible rockstars.

Anna Quindlen, a Pulitzer Prize-winning columnist for *The New York Times*, wrote in her book *Loud and Clear*, "I wish I had not been in such a hurry to get on to the next thing: dinner, bath, book, bed. I wish I had treasured the doing a little more and the getting it done a little less."[1]

The struggle is real, and while we could pretend that it's not that hard, let's face it: *It's hard*. But we know that work is a gift from God. Genesis 2:15 tells us, "The LORD God took the man and put him in the garden of Eden to work it and keep it" (ESV). We want to work like God is our boss. Additionally, Colossians 3:23-24 says, "Whatever you do, work heartily, as for the Lord and not for men, knowing that from the Lord you will receive the inheritance as your reward. You are serving the Lord Christ" (ESV).

We also know that God has placed relationships around us to impact and pour into for His kingdom—many times, that's our families. And that is a serious responsibility. This isn't lost on most. Most of us feel this tension, but we don't know how to resolve it.

Because of the flexibility I'm able to enjoy in my job, many days, I take my younger son, Silas, to school. Driving onto the school campus with him in the backseat fills me with so much joy. Some mornings he's quiet and leans his head against the window as his breath fogs up the glass. Other mornings, he chatters on about one thing or another all the way to school, and it's such a delight to me. Now that I have a son in high school as well, I'm starting to truly realize that the days are long but the years are short, and I grasp that I don't even know the half of that truth yet.

Just last night from the time of my writing this, I stayed up later than usual with my high schooler to help him study for a Spanish test.

"Okay, James. *Delante de*," I said.

James was exhausted from school, baseball, and a couple hours of homework from his ninth-grade honors classes.

He sighed as he laid his head back on the couch and closed his eyes. "I can't remember, Mom." He rubbed his temples. "I can't remember that one."

As a mom and study helper, I'm always looking for a trick to help as a memory aid. The week's words to memorize in Spanish were *in front*, *behind*, *on top of*, *below*, *between*, *with*, and *without*—tricky! Because they all are very similar to each other in Spanish.

Then, I had a lightbulb moment and said in an excited, high-pitched and squeaky, albeit tired, voice, "James! I've got it—*delante de*. *Delante* has an *l* in it. Like *l* for *lawn*. Your front lawn. Your front lawn is in front of your house. *Delante de* is 'in front of'—like your front lawn is in front of your house."

James stared at me blankly. It was 10:30 p.m., and we were both exhausted. I'd already looked over a geography PowerPoint about France, destroyed crepes in the kitchen that James and I were trying to make together (thank goodness for Dad's cooking and baking gifting and that he took over that situation), and then we were on to Spanish.

James and I burst out laughing. I knew this memory trick was terrible. I thought, *Maybe it was so terrible he would actually remember it.* Because it nearly makes no sense.

"Okay, Mom," James said, nodding once he stopped laughing. Some of his hair flopped into his eyes, but I could see his eyes roll thinking of how ridiculous Mom's study tricks could be. "Got it. *L* for *lawn*—your front lawn—*delante de*."

This is a typical evening at our house with me as a working mom. Flexibility helps the juggle. I know moments are passing that I will never get back with James and Silas. I also know prioritizing my marriage is important because once our kids soar on their own, Landon and I will be left to hang out for the remainder of our lives, and we want that time to be mostly a delight.

Staying as organized as possible helps keep things moving like a well-oiled machine. Keeping my work calendar with all our family's personal appointments intermixed is vital to me being able to remember what's happening and when. This ensures, with my work responsibilities, that I have the same task or due date in several places so that if I drop a ball in one spot, I'll catch myself up in another spot. Sometimes that means blocking a calendar appointment for work time on my own that is dedicated to *my* tasks that need completion, color coding that calendar appointment, setting a reminder, and sometimes even listing it on a spreadsheet. I know it sounds repetitive, but this kind of diligence has saved my life more than once. Also, I'm an over communicator. I communicate early and often to set expectations with clients and colleagues, and this gives me such peace of mind.

Making the most of the time I do have—maximizing ten minutes here or there—is a must. If I'm reading a book to help me professionally, I carry it around like the *Peanuts* character Linus carries around his blanket. Carpool line? I'm reading. Waiting for baseball to end? I have my laptop open and I am logged in answering a few emails.

And sure, I fall on the couch around 9:00 in the evening and am thankful to turn my brain off for just a few minutes before diving into bed.

It's a lot.

But you know what? I wouldn't change a thing. Except, maybe having my office be closer to home. If given the opportunity to start again, I would make all the same choices because this is what God has called me to—mom-ing, wife-ing, financial advisor-ing, and all the while, making His name known.

He's called you to the same: Making a kingdom impact. You may be in a different season of life, or have different roles or responsibilities, but rest in knowing—if God has called us, He will equip us. I pray we'll hear a voice behind us saying, "This is the way. Walk in it." And it will be the Holy Spirit. When your exhausted head hits your cold, soft pillow at night, rest well knowing you've given the day your all. Tomorrow will be a new day with new mercies. New challenges and new blessings. As my kids have grown, I've continually prayed that God would allow me to live in the present. To focus on the here and now. To eke out the most from every single wonderful moment of each season. God has called me to work outside our home and He has called me to be a mom. And I can do both and feel at peace that He is with me.

So, just as Jeff asked me, I now must ask you.

"Do you have a dream?"

And if you don't know, simply take just one step. It might start with stewarding your finances well and with intentionality, but it doesn't end there. Just be willing to ask our Savior, "Jesus, do You have a dream for me? Do You have a plan for my life that is far more than I could ask or imagine if I'm willing to trust You? Will You show me?"

I promise you, His answer is yes.

3

You Are a Caretaker

Learning to Steward Your Everything

If I could, I would shield and shelter my two boys from all pain. I would wrap them up tight, cozy and safe, in a big cocoon. I would throw them on my back and secure the ends of the cocoon around my front. So tight that it makes my fingers red from pulling the knots. I would talk to them, sing to them, and feed them when they were hungry. When my shoulders and back became tired, I would swing the cocoon around and carry them for a while in the front. I would look at how perfect they are, and I would tell them how much I love them a bazillion times every day. I would keep them only for me—for my great delight. I would keep them safe and completely whole, and anytime they outgrew my cocoon, I would simply make a bigger one.

I am overdramatizing this, but after all, isn't that what good mothers do? (*Can you hear the helicopter?*) Thus far, my children have remained extremely healthy. They have been darn near perfect. They've been sick at times, but have improved quickly, and all has been right with the world. Years ago, when one of them had croup, I couldn't sleep because I was straining to hear the baby monitor—already turned up to level five. I didn't want to miss a sound. I would sometimes think of smothering Landon with a pillow if he snored when one of the boys was sick, for fear I would miss any tiny sound signaling that I was needed. But humbly, throughout my journey of motherhood, I have been continually reminded that I am simply a caretaker for my children, and that we are called to steward our children, and truly, our everything, for God and His kingdom.

Now, looking back at photos, I realize I entered an awkward phase when my mom cut my hair into a mullet around the time I was in kindergarten; and I stayed in that awkward phase for many years (until the CHI hair straightener came out, and my whole life changed—that was in college). Eye glasses came into the picture for me when I was in second grade. In eighth grade, I switched schools, and I became a user of contacts rather than glasses. This too was just as life-altering, and I loved the change. I still wear contacts, for nearsightedness, and my vision is terrible. If I take my contacts out, I cannot even see the front of my hand.

Normally, I sleep in my contacts, but recently I had to get up in the middle of the night (it began to storm and I needed to do a "check" on everything), and I forgot I'd taken out my contacts. I couldn't see *anything*. At first, I thought something was terribly wrong with me. It wasn't, thank goodness, and I had to put on my glasses to see two inches in front of my face. Imperfect. I am imperfect. And pretty quickly into motherhood, I found out my children are imperfect as well. My imperfections I can live with, but theirs? Nope. I desire to carry those babies softly through life in my safe cocoon, for them to feel no pain, to not get made fun of, to feel no discomfort—only joy, peace, love, hope, and all the good experiences of life.

After Silas was born, at our first pediatrician visit after leaving the hospital, the doctor asked us about his right eye. She mentioned that it looked like he had ptosis (a drooping or falling of the upper eyelid). This is a condition a person is born with. But the doctor said what she was observing could also have been caused by his delivery or how he was lying in utero. There was still some swelling in his face, so we waited. A couple of weeks later, when we returned, she determined that, indeed, she thought he might have ptosis, and she sent us to a pediatric ophthalmologist.

Fast-forward almost two years. We had been seeing our incredibly wonderful pediatric ophthalmologist every three months, pretty much the whole of Silas's little life. And, as he neared two years old, at an appointment where she dilated his eyes, she told me he was nearsighted, and it was close to the point of him needing glasses. I was shocked. Why was I shocked? I don't know. Millions of people wear glasses—including me. *Hello*, genetics.

However, I had not considered this for my child. I thought, *My child is in my cocoon and should not have issues like ptosis or nearsightedness.* She let me know that day he would wear glasses, and probably fairly soon depending on how his nearsightedness progressed. Three months later she dilated his eyes again. His vision had worsened.

I cried.

I cried because he was falling out of my cocoon, and I was desperately trying my best to stuff him back in. I cried because I was the one who had passed on nearsightedness to him. By my reaction, you would have thought that I believed it was leprosy. I cried because I was worried he couldn't see well and I wanted him to experience everything on this beautiful earth in its fullest glory. The ophthalmologist said we could wait. But our next appointment was looming.

Sure enough, at that next appointment, we got Silas a pair of test glasses. His first pair of glasses. He was two years and three months old. The glasses had a strap around the back that kept them on his head because they were rubber and wouldn't stay on without the strap. We paid for anti-glare and anti-scratch. He tried them on, and he was so cute I could not stand it. We chose navy blue. I didn't cry. I wanted to, and I cried at home a little, but I was emotionally prepared. I asked a lot of questions. Good ones. How do you know if the prescription is not an overcorrection since he can't read an eye chart? Is it possible some kids really need glasses at this age, but they don't happen to be at an eye doctor (for ptosis like Silas), and so they don't find out about their problem until they enter kindergarten? Do we still need to patch Silas's eye to treat the ptosis? Does he need to wear his glasses all the time?

Silas fell out of my cocoon that day. I would have taken on his nearsightedness myself if I could have. I would have touched his eyes to heal them and blinded my own if I could have kept him in my cocoon of perfection. However, I couldn't.

That was the day I was gently reminded by the Holy Spirit, "Bethany, precious daughter, Silas is mine, and you are his caretaker. I hold him in My hand. You holding him in your 'cocoon' is an illusion. You can protect him, somewhat, as his parent, but I am in control of his life. I love him far more than you do—which I realize is unfathomable to you. Just as I love you far more than you can fathom. Silas is safe. He is protected. He is living in a fallen world, and his life will experience the result of that—physical imperfections, painful relationships, brokenness. I will walk with him, just as I have walked with you. I do not promise to right all wrongs on this earth right now, but I promise a relationship, and I promise Silas will never, ever walk alone."

The fact is, just as I am called to steward my everything, Silas is called to steward his everything.

Silas's glasses came in about a week after the big appointment. He sat on Landon's lap in the optician's chair and stared at himself in the mirror with wonder. He giggled and made faces, and he touched the glasses frame all the way around with his chubby little hands. I felt a little lighter as I loosened the knot on my protective cocoon and massaged my shoulders and neck where they had been clenched tightly to help clutch my babies in my perfect world. Silas began to wear glasses, and he was the cutest two year old I had ever seen with his sweet glasses. Maybe he didn't fall out of the cocoon that day after all. Perhaps he broke free like a butterfly learning to spread its wings.

Now, like back then, I still have a lot of work to do on my cocoon. The work of letting go of what I've placed inside it. For me, whatever I place in the cocoon becomes an idol. In God's loosening of my knots, in my standing in an open posture to Him, in remembering that God is good, and in however He sees fit to show my boys His goodness, I will trust. I will trust. I will trust. He is a good, good Father.

And God calls each of us to steward our everything. When it's easy. When it's hard. When life feels perfect. When life feels imperfect, and we carry the weight of this fleeting world in the most oppressive ways.

Silas isn't mine. As his parent, I am his caretaker, but he's not mine. And neither are my other family members. And neither are my clients. And neither is anyone else I want to kindly control and pretend to be the Holy Spirit over. I can attempt to live under an illusion of control for short spans of time, but I am reminded time and time again—as I imagine you are as well—that God wants our full *yes* on the table. He desires for us to steward our everything.

Stewarding Our Financial Everything

Many times, stewarding our everything starts with a willingness to engage in areas in which we feel less confident. Sometimes, that's our finances. In marriage, commonly, one spouse in the relationship is the financially minded spouse and the other person is the non-financially minded spouse. This means one of us is jazzed about spreadsheets and can't wait to file the taxes each year (that's me), and the other spouse never thinks for a minute about budgets or the Internal Revenue Service.

Individually, God has wired each of us, on purpose, with gifts and abilities and strengths and weaknesses. And if finances aren't what gets us out of bed each morning, money responsibilities, budgeting, or investing can begin to seem like an enigma. A foreign world we must avoid at all costs. But if God has told us He owns it all, and if He asks us to wisely steward all He has entrusted to us, then the financial piece of the puzzle is a part of that, and it is unwise to avoid it.

So practically, in the world of finances, what does stewarding our everything look like?

- Are we wisely managing the money we earn or receive each year?
- Do we know God's plan for us in the area of our finances?
- Do we have a spending plan, or does our money just seem to disappear?
- Do we have a giving plan that is in line with the way God has blessed us in our income and present situation?

Deuteronomy 8:18 says, "You are to remember the LORD your God, for it is He who is giving you power to make wealth" (NASB). Leaning into finances—opening the door to being a wise steward—can look like:

- If single, being willing to educate yourself on a basic level about spending, saving, giving, and investing
- If married, being open in your relationship to truly express a desire to collaborate in financial matters, rather than leaving the heavy responsibility on the shoulders of your spouse

An Invitation

Recently, we had an inquiry come in through our Blue Trust website. The questionnaire seemed to indicate the gentleman who submitted the inquiry was unmarried. When I contacted him, during our conversation, he eventually happened to mention something about his wife. This was an *aha!* moment for me because all other signs pointed to him being single. When I gently pressed for further details regarding his wife, he said something like, "She has nothing to do with our finances. She's not interested. I handle this aspect of our lives." I was taken aback by these words, as Blue Trust has a 45-year history of ensuring both spouses are included in each meeting from the very beginning of our relationship with clients. Because of that, this particular instance was quite unusual. But I respectfully listened, and we continued our conversation.

As a result of our discussion, this individual decided to become a financial planning and investment management client. And after working for about a month behind the scenes on a financial plan, we set a date for a Zoom meeting. I was prayed up and ready the day I asked him if he would mind if I invited his wife to attend our financial plan delivery meeting. He was kind but scoffed a bit at the idea and said, "You can invite her, but she won't be interested."

I had already begun including his wife in my email communications and then emailed her directly, cc'ing her husband, to ask if she'd be willing to join us. I shared how important it is for us to include a husband and wife—equally—in our meetings together. That in most cases, in most households, there is a financial spouse and a nonfinancial spouse, and they both bring equal value and worth to the marriage. I let her know that even if she didn't bring spreadsheet knowledge to our meeting, she would bring her heart knowledge and would be a valuable contributor. She agreed to think about it.

The meeting day arrived, and I logged into Zoom. Lo and behold, the second Zoom box to appear (I was the first) was this sweet wife. She seemed a little timid, but she showed up! The husband appeared a minute later, joining us from work.

After I opened our meeting in prayer and asked the Holy Spirit to enter into our time like a mighty rushing wind, I asked the couple,

"What's top of mind today? I would love for you to share anything on your hearts and minds as we begin our time together."

The husband jumped in to share, and in the second Zoom square, I could see the wife begin to cry. Not an out-of-control wailing, but from a place of genuine emotion. When the husband finished sharing, I tenderly asked the wife, "I can see there are some emotions on the surface this morning as we get started. Would you be willing to share with us what you're feeling?"

Her initial response was, "I don't know why I'm crying."

Her husband jumped back in and shared for a few more minutes regarding items he wanted to accomplish during the meeting time. Before I dove in, I paused for a moment and asked the wife—just once more—if there was anything she'd like to share.

And this time, she did.

She said something like, "I've never been invited into a financial meeting for our family before. I'm not sure why that makes me so emotional, and I know I don't know anything about finances, but I think I'm just overwhelmed to have simply been invited in."

The value and worth she felt on that meeting day had *nothing* to do with numbers or spreadsheets or eMoney software projections. It simply had to do with being invited into the conversation.

I pray that this wife will continue to feel valued and worthy and will become a confident contributor to our meetings together. It was clear she desired to steward her everything, and she simply needed someone to invite her in. She needed someone to encourage her and to communicate that she absolutely could do this and that she can be educated and equipped.

God-Given Stewardship

Ron Blue, the founder of Blue Trust, believes that stewardship is the use of God-given resources for the accomplishment of God-given goals. It is careful and responsible management of something entrusted to one's care. It's utilizing and managing all resources God provides for His glory and for the betterment of His creation. And, it's managing everything that God brings into our lives in a manner that honors Him. God is not as concerned about the amount we have as He is about our use and management of that amount. This is very clear in the parable of the talents found in Matthew 25:14-30. I love the way *The Message* shares this story:

> It's also like a man going off on an extended trip. He called his servants together and delegated responsibilities. To one he gave five thousand dollars, to another two thousand, to a third one thousand, depending on their abilities. Then he left. Right off, the first servant went to work and doubled his master's investment. The second did the same. But the man with the single thousand dug a hole and carefully buried his master's money.
>
> After a long absence, the master of those three servants came back and settled up with them. The one given five thousand dollars showed him how he had doubled his investment. His master commended him: "Good work! You did your job well. From now on be my partner."
>
> The servant with the two thousand showed how he also had doubled his master's investment. His master commended him: "Good work! You did your job well. From now on be my partner."
>
> The servant given one thousand said, "Master, I know you have high standards and hate careless ways, that you demand the best and make no allowances for error. I was afraid I might disappoint you, so I found a good hiding place and secured your money. Here it is, safe and sound down to the last cent."

> The master was furious. "That's a terrible way to live! It's criminal to live cautiously like that! If you knew I was after the best, why did you do less than the least? The least you could have done would have been to invest the sum with the bankers, where at least I would have gotten a little interest."
>
> "Take the thousand and give it to the one who risked the most. And get rid of this 'play-it-safe' who won't go out on a limb. Throw him out into utter darkness."

At the end of my life, I hope Landon and I are sitting in rocking chairs on our front porch on a cool day, watching our grandchildren play in our yard. As I rock back and forth in a steady rhythm, I'll think of the legacy I will leave and the past choices I've made. I will always have regrets because we are living in a fallen and broken world. But as I look back, I want to have as few regrets as possible. I want to know that, with intentionality, I stewarded my everything for God's glory. That I left nothing on the table. That I held nothing back.

At the end of the day, I am responsible for stewarding what God has entrusted to me and handling it to bring honor to Him and accomplish His purposes. To do this, I can't trust in myself. I can convince myself of anything. Thus the need for biblically solid instruction, coaching, accountability, partnership, and guidance in my own life. The more I have and the richer I am, the more critical this accountability becomes. We will all stand before God and give an account. And we want to hear, "Well done, good and faithful servant. You have been faithful over a little; I will set you over much" (Matthew 25:21 ESV).

Like my client's wife, who was thankful to be invited into a financial discussion for the first time, engagement in the process and accountability will lead to peace of mind.

Just as I tried (and failed) to hold my children in my cocoon of safety, I invite you to take some time and ask the Father to reveal what you are clutching in your cocoon. Is it your job? Your family? Your fear of failing to walk in confidence with finances? Your own cemented ideas about who you are and who you're not, and who you believe you could never be?

Did you know that 94 percent of women believe they will need to be personally responsible for their finances at some point in their lives?[1] Whether they want to or not, and whether they feel prepared to or not. In addition, only 28 percent of women actually feel empowered to take action in the area of finances.[2]

These statistics are concerning because it means 72 percent of us do not feel empowered or equipped to take action. We don't know our own worth. And while financial education is extremely important—breaking down seemingly complicated concepts into bite-sized actions—I truly believe, with women, how we view ourselves plays into these statistics. Do we believe we're capable? Do we truly believe we have value? Do we know that God has placed each of us on this earth with a purpose that no one else can accomplish? Do we realize we're invited in, already fully loved and accepted, and that we have a seat at the table? We have a reserved seat at the table. It's a seat no one else can fill but you.

I invite you to loosen the knots of whatever you're holding tightly. Come on, you can do it! I see those white knuckles as you clutch your comfort zone. This is a safe space. Unclasp your hands as slowly as you need to. This is a place of grace. Move one small step at a time as God leads. Let go of idols that are holding you back from what God has for you. Be willing to walk into whatever you're afraid of. Whatever you don't believe you're capable of. That's where God does His best work. You simply must because that's what stewards do. They're bold. They're courageous. They leave nothing on the table. Watch and see what God does when you steward your everything.

4

You Can Do Hard Things

Steering Clear of Debt and Making Wise Investments

A number of years ago, my boys took survival swimming lessons. These specialized lessons were called ASI, or Aquatic Survival Instruction. The boys had to pass a test at the end of the lessons so they could graduate. They checked off certain skills, which included exercises like falling into the water dressed in full winter attire—coats and all. Another one involved Silas being tossed into the water near James to see what his brother would do if a crisis situation arose.

Silas, my Rocky Balboa, immediately took to these lessons. In fact, he even chose to continue swimming lessons a good while longer. After completing ASI, he learned side breathing and the backstroke.

James, however, didn't love the lessons as much. He *really* didn't love them. Because he was the older brother, he never pitched an all-out fit, but because he was eight years old at the time and I was insisting we get this "swimming" thing down, he was not pleased. Sometimes, there were even some tears shed in the pool during his lessons.

James is very smart, and he is such a rule follower on top of being a tenderhearted kid. He's athletic, but something about swimming wasn't great for him. He didn't like holding his breath underwater and he didn't like his head being under the surface either. The instructors worked diligently with him. They taught him breathing exercises, and with great patience, we went week by week and survived. James learned, and eventually, along with Silas, three months after beginning the lessons, James graduated.

That was a big deal.

Why?

Because we can do hard things. Especially when we have people around us—supporting us, cheering us on, and believing in us. That's when we can most definitely do hard things. I felt like this was my chant to him during those three tough months: "Even if you think you can't, I'll tell you again. You can do hard things, Buddy."

He could. And he did.

James was successful, and I pray he learned a valuable life lesson through that experience. When I want to quit, instead, I press in. I take a step forward. I let people help hold up my arms (figuratively, clearly not while swimming) and encourage me while spurring me on to greatness.

Because I can do hard things.

As adults, sometimes it seems like life is rolling along fine, and then, a huge dumpster fire ignites. We are just trying to survive a hard thing that is chasing us down. Thoughts of James's courage and bravery pushed me on to success when I experienced a hard season the year after those swimming lessons.

Around the same time James and Silas began their ASI lessons, I began my own journey, a journey to seek my Certified Financial Planner® certification. I'd been at Blue Trust for 11 years, serving in different roles and divisions, and I clearly felt God was telling me to work on this certification. With the incredibly important support of my boss, Jeff, and my other team members, I began the one-and-a-half-year journey of coursework, studying, and testing.

Once I completed the coursework and began exam preparation, my life turned upside down. I worked *hard.* The exam was fast approaching, so I put my head down and studied every possible moment. With my travel coffee mug as my best friend, I listened to CFP® podcasts on my hour-long commute to work each morning. I studied exam prep materials when I arrived at work an hour early and practiced quizzes for an hour at lunch. I worked on my flashcards during my hour-long commute home each day. And on the weekends? I studied. Landon took the boys. I felt guilty. Guilty about whether I was good enough as a mom and wife. Guilty about the help Landon was giving me. And I was unsure of whether I was even smart enough to get through the challenge.

The exam date came. Normally, candidates receive their score right away, but because of test questions that covered brand new legislation, the scores were delayed. So I waited anxiously. And, on a dreary Wednesday evening three weeks and two days after taking the exam, I was pulling on my pajamas to head to bed for the night when I heard my phone vibrate. I walked over to the cherrywood dresser where the phone sat to check the notification. With bewildered eyes, I read the email in disbelief. Once. Twice. Three times.

I did not pass.

It said something like, "I'm sorry to report you were unsuccessful in your attempt..."

Just. Yuck.

My face immediately fell, my heart dropped, and my eyes blurred with tears. I had studied for more than 250 hours during the three months leading up to the test. I took a live review. I did every single thing that I knew I could do to prepare. I made a lot of sacrifices. My family made a lot of sacrifices.

And it just wasn't enough. It felt like *I* wasn't enough. And then, God brought to mind James and those swimming lessons.

And I knew...

"I can do hard things." I spoke these words out loud, if only to hear them for myself and believe they were true.

The day after I found out I'd been unsuccessful, I jumped right back in the saddle. I paid for an upgraded review and began studying again. I drank more coffee (with peppermint mocha creamer, of course). Landon stepped in closer instead of stepping out in anger and frustration, though I know he must have felt some of that inside. He supported me even more. And at Blue Trust, where my work family could have given up on me and just said, "Forget it," they stepped in too. They pulled me in to let me shadow their work even more and continued to offer to help me in any way.

When hard things became harder, people didn't step back...they dug in. *We* dug in together, because I wasn't alone.

I retook the six-hour exam four months later, when it was offered again. By the end of the test, when I clicked submit, I had no idea whether I'd passed. The exam was just that hard for me, and many of the questions felt extremely subjective. Instead of receiving a preliminary pass/fail on my computer screen, I was to receive one by email immediately after the exam (an upgrade since the first time I took the test). As I rose from my desk chair in the testing center to turn in my scratch paper and pencils, I was shaking so badly I was afraid I would pass out. I removed my few personal items from my assigned locker, and I tried to breathe on the way to the car. I took each step on the sidewalk intentionally, reminding myself that my worth is not in the CFP® certification. Who I am is not up for debate—my value is not negotiable or earned.

I climbed into my gray Honda Odyssey van on the bottom level of the parking garage, laid my head back against the headrest, and took a few deep breaths. The email had come. But instead of repeating the same words from last time, it said:

"Congratulations! A preliminary analysis of your test results shows that you were successful in achieving the passing standard established by the CFP® Board..."

And I began to cry. I began to cry an ugly cry in the ugliest way possible. I called Landon, who was in the dentist's office waiting to have his teeth cleaned.

Through ugly tears, I told him, "I passed. I could never have made the journey without you."

Then, I called my parents—both of them separately at their respective jobs. And then, I called my coworkers and bosses. I knew it would feel like the way it did, like I, alone, did not receive the CFP® certification, but we all earned it together.

I have been through some heartbreaking times in my adult life, times when I was unsure about a lot of things. My CFP® journey wasn't a soul-searching time like those, but it was hard. It was a challenge. And I had a choice. I had a choice as to whether I would sit in failure, or if I would allow others to hold my arms up and encourage me to keep going. I kept going, and I did a hard thing.

Just like James—though I hope I'm never thrown in a pool with my winter coat on—I pushed forward, did some breathing exercises, and persevered.

We can *definitely* do hard things.

Steering Clear of Debt

Many times, the Lord has shown me this truth over the years, just as He did the day Hailey shuffled into my office for our ten o'clock meeting. She seemed fidgety and nervous, as if I was about to ask her to walk on a bed of hot coals. I smiled reassuringly. "Hi, Hailey. Why don't you take a seat?" I gestured toward the chair on the other side of my desk. "Can I get you coffee or a soda?"

"No, thank you." She did sit down, but she desperately clutched the tattered green notebook she'd brought in with her.

I knew Hailey was anxious about our meeting—in fact, she'd probably rather have been at the dentist having bitewing x-rays—but I didn't realize how scared she was. Her near panic was palpable as I asked the Lord to help me calm her fears and let her know she was fully accepted and valued no matter her financial situation.

Just as I do in most meetings, after praying to kick off our time together, I leaned forward and asked her what was top of mind. "Hailey, I'm very thankful you are sitting here in this chair in my office today. I truly believe God ordains every single relationship, and it's no accident that you and I are getting to know each other. I'm looking forward to diving into whatever God has for us. Why don't you share what's on your heart today as we begin our time together?"

I could see Hailey's hands shaking as she avoided eye contact. She reached up and smoothed her hair, then cleared her throat and continued to look down, staring at her shoes.

She hesitated so long before speaking that I was unsure if she was going to actually begin saying words.

"Well, Bethany, I'm basically just a hot mess, and I am weary," she blurted out. "I earn a good salary, and on paper, I should be able to cover my needs and many of my wants, but I keep ending up in debt. It seems like I can never get out of it." Wringing her hands, she continued. "I've even begun pulling from some of my investment accounts to pay debts, and I know that's unsustainable. It's like, as I anticipate paying off one debt, I choose to take on another debt, and I just keep doing the same thing over and over again, all the while hoping something will change. I recognize that's the definition of insanity—doing the same thing over and over again and anticipating a different result. The thing is, I'm embarrassed, and I don't even know why I'm here today. I'm an adult, and I need to just stop it."

The shroud of shame over Hailey's entire body was nearly tangible. My eyes filled with tears as I tenderly looked across the desk at this beautiful woman of God. It was clear this cycle of debt was not just a practical piece of her puzzle but an unspoken belief about who she was as a person, as a child of God.

Do any of the following thoughts sound familiar?

- *Oh, I'm not any good with money. It's not my thing.*
- *Debt is part of life. Everyone has it.*
- *I'm good at some things, but investing isn't one of them.*
- *I can stop taking on debt anytime I want. I just don't think it's a big deal.*
- *I really can't manage a budget—my mind doesn't work that way.*

And all the while, overlaid on top of these messages are feelings of shame, inferiority, and wanting to hide. Scrambling to portray a calm and "together" image while falling apart inside. Running as fast as we can to keep the imaginary wheel spinning, but inside we're utterly exhausted. Tired of running. Tired of worrying. Tired of the same old patterns.

Dear reader, please allow me to gently remind you—*you* can do hard things.

Maybe it's not swimming lessons.

Maybe it's not the CFP® exam.

But maybe it's surviving life moment to moment right now, because things are really hard.

Maybe it's learning to live within your means and not taking on a debt.

There's always hope. There's always a next right step.

As a believer, I recognize that maturing financially sometimes can mean foregoing present desires for future rewards and benefits. While the Bible never says that debt is a sin, it does say, in Proverbs 22:7, that "the borrower is slave to the lender." We become preoccupied by our debts. Continually borrowing and staying in a cycle of debt sentences us to a more financially constrained lifestyle in the future. Debt, simply stated, is a contract to pay later for what we receive now.

Using debt unwisely and inappropriately can create a barrier to our reliance on God and our freedom to respond to His call. Taking on debt impacts us spiritually, economically, psychologically, and personally—whether we realize it or not. Hence, Hailey's shroud of shame. Her hesitancy to share her situation. Her feelings of inadequacy and unworthiness.

If we are married, these are sometimes some of the toughest conversations to step into with our spouse. Being a woman of worth takes bravery and boldness as we share truth (with grace and respect) and allow ourselves to be vulnerable with our husbands to lay out how the Holy Spirit may be speaking to us in the area of debt. Many times, this looks like asking questions such as, "Should we take on this debt?" and "If so, why?"

As I look back on some of my own marriage conversations, decisions about debt have been some of our most uncomfortable discussions. Ladies, we must choose to push through awkwardness and discomfort—our contributions to God's kingdom and the legacy we will leave are at stake!

How do we gain confidence in this area and begin to make wise decisions?

First and foremost, we must allow the Father to take away the shame and indictment of who we believe we are. Ask Him to show us who we are in His eyes. We are fully loved and accepted—we couldn't be more loved and accepted—whether we're in debt or debt-free. There's no extra love for those who have plenty of money in savings.

Second, let's consider the following wisdom: If an item will decline in value after purchase, it's not the best choice to use debt to buy it. Clothes, food, electronics, and even cars are just a few examples. Many times, it's purchases like these that cause us to step into a cycle of debt from which it's hard to climb out of. Most of the time, we would call these purchases consumer debt. Using credit cards to purchase items we can't pay off in the same month, taking on vehicle loans for cars we can't afford, and just generally moving in certain directions before God has provided.

Don't Presume Upon the Future

When we use debt unwisely, we are presuming upon the future by assuming everything will go just as we've planned. Perhaps we look forward to an increased salary, or windfall of an inheritance we're expecting (you know, one day), or count on future investment returns that are projected to be off the charts.

James 4:13-15 says, "Listen, you who say, 'Today or tomorrow we will go to this or that city, spend a year there, carry on business and make money.' Why, you do not even know what will happen tomorrow. What is your life? You are a mist that appears for a little while and then vanishes. Instead, you ought to say, 'If it is the Lord's will, we will live and do this or that.'"

To be an effective steward, we must focus more on living a manageable lifestyle today and rely less on what the future may hold.

Be Willing to Wait

Ugh, this principle is difficult, isn't it? In our culture of Amazon, Door Dash, and InstaCart, I get really aggravated if the groceries I ordered or the item I "need" won't arrive within a convenient window of time. Or, if I need to wait more than two days for the item. I recognize there are some times in our lives when we absolutely cannot wait for a need that has arisen. But many times, we *can* wait. I *can* wait for the yellow tablecloth I just ordered that matches my cute lemon tree centerpiece. I *can* wait for the next cute crochet kit I've had my eye on. I have the choice of holding off on ordering the next new release written by my favorite novelist. I. Can. Wait.

Here is a list of thought-provoking questions to ask before taking on a debt:

- Have I prayed about taking on the debt?
- Do I have a guaranteed source of repayment?
- Will the debt cause me to lessen my current charitable giving?
- Will repaying debt mean having to work more hours?
- What need is this debt meeting that cannot be met otherwise?
- Does the debt make economic sense (borrowing for a house versus a car)?
- If married, do my spouse and I agree on the debt?
- Will the debt reduce current funding of other goals (like retirement accounts or other major savings goals)?
- Can I wait and see what God does to provide first?
- Is this debt short-circuiting what God may want to provide in His time?

In a world that tells us to give up quickly, seek immediate gratification (after all, "we deserve it!"), and take the path of least resistance, God calls us to take a higher road. A road that requires us to do hard things and make wise decisions. A road paved with full reliance on Him as He guides and directs our paths. Remember, we can do hard things!

Making Wise Investments

Growing up, I had a love-hate relationship with math. I did well in math class some years, and in other years I struggled—like in geometry (just stop it!).

In my second year of college, as I plodded steadily toward graduating with a bachelor of science in business administration, I took business calculus with professor Julia Polk. I expected to suffer through it in order to check off a box. Surprisingly, I entered a whole new world of word problems that I actually enjoyed solving. Professor Polk not only knew her content well, but she was gifted in teaching that content to students. This was a whisper from the Lord that I might enjoy doing math in the real world.

But it wasn't "math" alone that excited me. It was money. Not having money, but handling money—actual dollars and cents. I remember begging my dad to let me count down the drawer at Wise Equipment Sales and Service, our family business that was our small town's Kubota and John Deere tractor dealership.

"Dad, pleeeeeeeease let me count down the drawer," I pleaded for the millionth time one evening after closing.

And finally, shockingly, he sighed an *I've-worked-all-day-and-I'm-exhausted* sigh that only a business owner knows, then he smiled and opened the cash drawer. He set the insert on the cold, smooth counter and began to school me on counting down the drawer.

The pennies, dimes, nickels, and quarters felt weighty as I slid each coin across the granite with my right hand and into the awaiting palm of my left hand.

As I began to take on more responsibility working part-time in our family business, I never took for granted that it was my duty to wisely steward Wise Equipment's money—even in counting down the drawer. Even in preparing the deposit the next morning as I drank my favorite Wise-Equipment Folger's coffee. Even in simply driving the deposit to the bank. I always recognized the honor in being trusted with someone else's funds.

Knowing how I'd loved to help with "money" tasks at Wise Equipment, it seemed a natural step for me to attempt to work at a bank when we moved to New Orleans for Landon to attend seminary. Even in being a teller (for only a short time before Katrina blew through), it was the same theme: money and relationships. Customers to care for and funds to steward.

Remember, money isn't good or bad—it is merely a tool. We know it all belongs to God, and we're called to wisely steward the resources He's entrusted to us. Part of that is learning to make wise investments.

Even the word *investments* can seem like an enigma. And, here's a word of reassurance: We don't have to become investment experts to invest wisely. If we learn to unmask the mystery and start simply, then education is our first step in gaining the confidence we need to take one step at a time in the right direction.

Investing plays an important role in the overall stewardship process to help us provide for our families, do good works, and be generous. Investments are considered a *tool* to assist us in accomplishing financial goals. They are a part of the planning process, not an end in themselves. We know that we accumulate wealth by spending less than we make over a long period of time and by preserving our wealth with investments. Wealth is not accumulated through investments alone. Let's take a pause to make sure that sinks in: Investments *preserve* our wealth. They do not *create* our wealth.

When determining how to invest wisely, individuals are usually guided by a couple of concepts that are seen in different life phases—accumulation and decumulation.

Accumulation

Many of us—including me—are in the accumulation phase of life. We're in the season of earning income and building wealth. During this stage, it can be helpful to use a guide called the Sequential Investment Strategy: Accumulation. This approach uses stairsteps to order our priorities as we attempt to wisely steward the resources God has provided to us.

These steps include:

1. Debt Payoff: Work diligently to aggressively pay off any non-mortgage debt, while also starting an emergency fund.

2. Emergency Reserves: Establish an emergency savings. If you

Sequential Investment Strategy: Accumulation

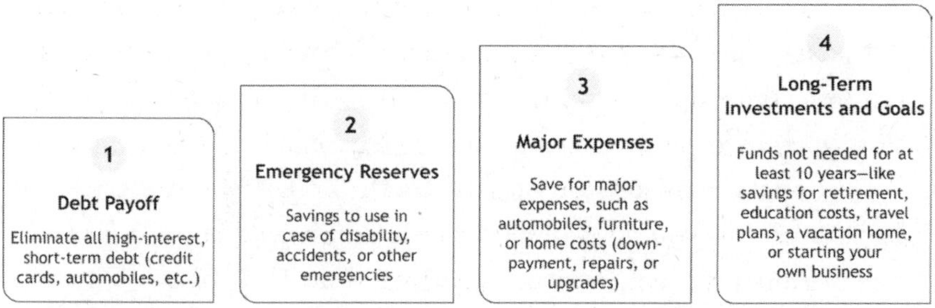

1	2	3	4
Debt Payoff	**Emergency Reserves**	**Major Expenses**	**Long-Term Investments and Goals**
Eliminate all high-interest, short-term debt (credit cards, automobiles, etc.)	Savings to use in case of disability, accidents, or other emergencies	Save for major expenses, such as automobiles, furniture, or home costs (down-payment, repairs, or upgrades)	Funds not needed for at least 10 years—like savings for retirement, education costs, travel plans, a vacation home, or starting your own business

are in your accumulation years, having around six months of emergency savings is a good target. If you are in a retirement season, having one to two years of expenses saved is wise. If you're just starting out, and six months seems insurmountable, begin with a smaller amount. Even only $1,000 saved makes a difference as you continue to add to this fund.

Balancing debt payoff and building an emergency savings at the same time can be tricky. While we desire to pay off debt as quickly as possible, we don't want to make the mistake of depleting our emergency savings so that if an emergency comes…well, you guessed it. More debt. This can become a vicious cycle.

While paying off nonmortgage debt (and really any debt) is a high priority, we must be careful to also save so that if an emergency happens (and we all know life happens—as my new $700 dryer waves to me from the laundry room as I type), we are prepared with cash. It's okay to steadily plod toward reducing debt based on priorities and even the debt's interest rate. But we should always, *always* be working toward debt payoff and have a goal of at least three to six months of living expenses in an emergency savings (and possibly more depending on your stage of life). This may not happen overnight. One step at a time is a huge victory!

3. Major Expenses: Create savings buckets to save for major upcoming expenses, such as home repairs, a home remodel, a home down payment, auto repairs, or a big trip. Many online banks allow you to create "buckets" or sub-accounts that separate and clearly identify your savings goals. As we discussed in chapter 2, these buckets can be a clarifying tool to show you what you're saving for and how close you are to accomplishing your savings goals.

4. Long-Term Investments and Goals: Long-term investments are investments you don't need to touch for at least ten years. These investments may include your 401(k), or Roth IRA, or even funds you've placed in a taxable investment account from extra savings that you know won't be needed for more than ten years.

It's very important that your long-term investments are well diversified. Diversifying means, very simply, not putting all your eggs in one basket. Would you believe me if I told you that the Bible speaks to this concept? Ecclesiastes 11:2 says, "Divide your portion to seven, or even to eight, for you do not know what misfortune may occur upon the earth" (NASB).

Some people believe diversification means placing their investments at a whole bunch of different well-known financial institutions. For example, clients I serve who have believed this in the past have come to me with accounts at Schwab, Fidelity, Vanguard, and other major institutions. They will have the exact same types of accounts at each of these companies, and they believe this is what being well diversified means. It *can* mean they are well diversified, but wow, how complicated!

But this can be simplified. You can place all your investments within one institution and still diversify the investments well. If you are managing your own investments (and not using an investment manager), an easy way to diversify your investments within an account can be to choose what is called a "target date fund." A target date fund allows you to select a fund matching a probable retirement date for you, and then, invests your funds aggressively and/or conservatively depending on the timeframe until the date you've selected.

Investments start out more aggressive, especially if the target date is a long way out, and become more conservative over time.

While target date funds aren't perfect, for an investor who is not interested in managing accounts often and closely, selecting a target date fund ensures diversity within accounts and appropriate risk. A lack of diversification shows why it can be dangerous to put all your retirement funds in one stock. It can seem successful if the stock is growing and thriving for a time, but when market cycles happen, as history shows us they do, the lack of diversity can bring devastation to what once may have seemed like a "sure thing." Many financial institutions can walk you through a series of questions that help you diversify your funds when you open an account.

If you don't know where to start, seek some wisdom from a trustworthy source.

Decumulation

Eventually, after being in the accumulation phase and following those stairsteps, you enter a decumulation phase—when you're figuring out how to wisely distribute the resources and funds you've earned and saved, or perhaps, even inherited. The decumulation phase is normally a later season in life when you may not be earning regular income from a job and want to ensure you are wisely positioning the funds you need to live and cover expenses now and in the coming years.

Sequential Investment Strategy: Decumulation

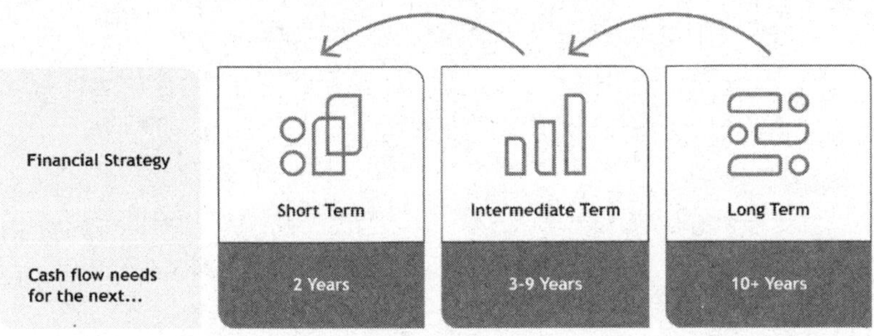

When the Blue Trust team thinks about positioning investments for the best success, we are always asking: What is the money for? and How long will it be until it is needed? The answers to these questions help guide us to make the best recommendations for each client's situation. Generally, we follow these guidelines:

- If you need the funds in the next one or two years, we suggest investing those funds in a very short-term, conservative investment vehicle—such as a high-yield savings or money market account. This would include your emergency fund and cash for major purchases you anticipate making in the next few years. While interest earned in high-yield savings and money market accounts fluctuates depending on the current economic environment, try to maximize earning as much as you can wherever you choose to park your savings funds.
- If you need the money in the next three to nine years, we call these intermediate-term investments. These are funds that have a goal to keep pace with inflation but normally do not have the volatility (or growth potential) that many long-term investments have. These options normally include bonds and bond-like investments.
- Finally, if you can allow the funds to grow for ten or more years before you need them, we recommend investing those funds for the long term in more equity-type investments. Depending on your age, many times, this looks like a retirement fund such as a 401(k), 403(b), IRA, or Roth IRA. Keep in mind that long-term investments can also be made in a taxable brokerage account. I love the idea of a well-diversified balance sheet, which means you may have several different types of long-term accounts. It is wise not to have all your money locked up

in retirement accounts that are taxable and usually have a penalty for early withdrawal. Instead, it is ideal to also have a nonretirement account, like a joint or individual taxable account, for long-term savings that is accessible without penalty before and after you retire. This strategy can also help you to manage your tax bracket during retirement (not always having to pull from taxable retirement accounts).

Now, if your mind is swirling with questions, good news, you're normal! God didn't create everyone to be an investment expert. We all swim in our own, God-determined lanes of giftedness and passion. Don't push yourself to be something you're not. But do recognize that you are capable of much more than you may give yourself credit for. If you're married, don't hesitate to jump in on investment conversations as you and your husband discuss where and how much to invest. Whether on your own through investigating wise resources or with the help of a trusted advisor, be encouraged that you have the ability to make wise investment choices. And the wisest investment choices are always, first and foremost, rooted in faith.

Investing with Purpose

Sharon, a practicing family physician for more than 30 years, sat down in one of our Blue Trust conference rooms with me, and I was overcome with delight at how down to earth she was. Todd, Sharon's husband, maintains their large farm while Sharon continues to serve individuals and families through her medical practice. After growing up in a small town and being immersed in my family's tractor business, encountering folks who remind me of home always fills me with joy. As Sharon dumped a truckload of paper statements in my lap, she began to share her heart.

"Bethany, I just want to invest my money in a way that honors God—a way that lines up with my beliefs and convictions." She sat in a nearby chair, her words tumbling forward faster than a zero-turn lawn mower. "All these years I've been investing, and I really don't even know what I'm investing in. I have no idea what I'm supporting! At this point, I feel such a burden in this area that I'm willing to sacrifice investment return if there's a way I can feel I'm making a difference."

Sharon isn't alone. Many of us, as Jesus followers, wrestle with the tension that can easily surface as we invest our hard-earned money into companies we know little to nothing about or have serious moral and ethical concerns with.

In finance, this is an area that has come very far, and guess what? We don't need to (and shouldn't need to) sacrifice returns to align our investments with our biblical convictions. At Blue Trust, we truly desire to support our clients in identifying and implementing strategies that support their convictions, faith, and values. More details on investing with this in mind are available in appendix A: "Financial Planning with Purpose" at the end of this book.

When it came to learning lessons about money, I got my start in the family business and couldn't have asked for a better training ground. Let me take you back to one of my favorite memories.

After walking in to Wise Equipment from the morning dew and humidity outside, my disposable foam cup felt sticky in my hands. As I poured the morning's coffee—brewed from the bathroom tap water—I thought about the day ahead. Adding powdered coffee creamer and Splenda, I said good morning to mechanics as I stepped out of the way for others to enjoy the life-giving brew. As I neared the office and took a right into the doorway, there was Bob. Quiet, like usual, but smiling because he knew I loved his coffee.

"Good today?" he grunted.

"Delicious! Mmm, mmmm!" I said enthusiastically, not really knowing if he meant the coffee or just how I was doing in general.

He nodded, grinned, and carried on in his quiet way.

My coffee—which was nothing more than powdered creamer and Splenda with a little coffee mixed in—was a part of my daily routine. The hot liquid was soothing as it ran down my throat, while my computer booted up for me to begin some of my mundane, but important, tasks. That cup sat beside me like a best friend as I stamped the checks from the night before, counted cash and coins again—this time with a printout from the ten-key adding machine—and finally folded everything together. I stapled the stack in the left corner only, as I'd been instructed when learning to complete these tasks.

Once the daily deposit was complete, so was the coffee. As I tossed the disposable cup into my garbage can and prepared to take the deposit to the bank, I had no idea that, years later, I would sit drinking coffee in the mornings while meeting with clients as a financial advisor. Stewarding more funds than I'd seen on an evening or morning at Wise Equipment, but working with the same integrity, the same heart, and the same cup of coffee (though, admittedly, no one makes it quite like Bob did).

Let me invite you to separate facts from fiction. There's no place for shame here. You are precious and treasured, and it's time to embrace it. No matter what your situation, there's a place to start, and you can do this. One step at a time. Steady plodding always comforts me. As is commonly said, "Rome wasn't built in a day, you know." Tell the critical voice in your head to check itself at the door, and let's get ready to steward our everything while we do hard things.

Whether tackling debt aggressively, paying attention to how your money is invested, or desiring to align your faith with your investments, this is your time. God knew you would be reading this material right now—at this very moment—and He has a plan for you and for me. I just hope it always includes coffee.

5

Your Life Overflowing

The Force of Generosity in a Self-Focused World

With a Whataburger french fry hanging out of my mouth, I stared at Matt in disbelief. What began as an innocuous invitation to fellowship after Sunday evening church suddenly turned into something altogether different. And I couldn't help but think of Matthew 6:19-21, "Do not lay up for yourselves treasures on earth, where moth and rust destroy and where thieves break in and steal; but lay up for yourselves treasures in heaven, where neither moth nor rust destroys and where thieves do not break in and steal. For where your treasure is, there your heart will be also" (NKJV).

When church ended on that particular Sunday evening, Landon and I stepped out of the glass doors of the building into a wall of stifling Florida humidity and headed to our car. But Matt stopped us.

"How about meeting me at Whataburger?" he yelled across the parking lot.

Landon and I turned to look at each other. You know, the look you give a close friend or significant other when something odd is happening. You can't let your face show it, but you're intrigued and confused.

While we knew Matt, a deacon at our church, we didn't know him well, and it was certainly a little odd that without notice we'd suddenly moved into a hanging-out-after-church relationship.

Landon and I shrugged and yelled across the parking lot, "Uh, sure! See you in a few minutes!"

On the ten-minute drive from our church to Whataburger, we created various scenarios of what Matt must have wanted to share with us. *Maybe he simply wants to pray with us*, we thought. Or perhaps he desired to give us his opinion on the direction of our lives. We were two years into marriage and had begun looking at homes in Slidell, Louisiana, in anticipation of our upcoming move for seminary. Our Crestview home had just been put under contract to sell, and we had a good ballpark figure for a price range as we began our Slidell home search.

We pulled into a parking space and climbed out of the car as we wondered what Matt wanted to discuss. And, what in the world was I going to eat at Whataburger since I'd never entered the restaurant in my life? Years later, I now know that Whataburger has what some jokingly call a cult following, but I was more naïve in those days and didn't have an appreciation for this in our small town.

Matt held the restaurant door open for us as we awkwardly stepped in and headed to the counter. Landon and I ordered french fries and a Coke, while Matt headed back to an orange booth to sit by the window without getting anything for himself.

Grabbing our bag of greasy fries and clutching our already sweating medium Coke, we slid onto the hard plastic bench across from Matt.

We didn't know this at the time, but Matt isn't one to mince words. He isn't someone who uses flowery language or polite niceties because that's how you're *supposed* to act. He speaks when he has something to say. He is authentic and very kind, and mostly just listens—taking in everything being said and internalizing it deeply.

So immediately, he cleared his throat and began to share.

"I've been praying for the two of you as you head to seminary. I know this is a big step, and Landon, I can't wait to see what God has ahead for you." Matt gave us a significant look. "As I've been praying, God has told me to give you $40,000."

Hard stop.

I don't know about you, but I'd be glad if someone told me they wanted to give me one dollar. Or five. Forty grand isn't exactly an amount on my radar…like, ever. But it was on God's radar.

Because, unbeknownst to Matt, a folded 8.5 by 11-inch piece of paper sat right beside me inside my gold-colored leather purse. And in my stunned state, all I could do was reach into my purse and pull out the piece of paper.

Remember when you had to print out documents before smartphones were a thing? When the internet existed at home or the office, but you had to print important information so you could carry it with you? That's exactly what we had done as we visited Slidell the week before to look at homes. We'd narrowed the homes down to one in particular—nothing spectacular and looking back, a bit sketchy—a property we could purchase and live in and make our own during the three years we anticipated Landon would attend seminary in New Orleans.

And on that Sunday night in the Whataburger booth, I pulled the piece of paper out of my purse, my hands shaking. I unfolded it and laid it on the table. And I had no words.

As we all looked down at the table, Landon and Matt could see what I already knew was there. A printed MLS real estate listing of the home we'd decided God was leading us to purchase. And at the top, in my handwriting, there was a number. A number written in pencil—the dollar amount I knew we would need for a mortgage after using the expected profits of our current home sale as a large down payment.

It was $40,000.

To this day, I can transport my mind right back to that booth in a flash. It was the first time I saw God act in an extremely specific way. The first time I saw Him tangibly say, "This is My plan, and I, the Lord, will make it happen. You follow. I'll lead. You obey. I'll provide. You walk. I'll make a way."

And make a way, He did. Through one man's radical generosity.

Most of us recognize that giving should be an integral part of any maturing Jesus follower's life. We know giving is commanded in Scripture both for the benefit of the recipient and for the benefit of the giver, and we must prayerfully determine the amount God requires of us. Giving should be done proportionately to one's income and should be done regularly and cheerfully.

Watching our clients give and seeing the unique ways the Lord calls each of us to make sacrifices to grow His kingdom is humbling and inspiring to watch. The amazing thing is that we each have a distinctive giving journey the Lord has called us to walk in. Mine is not yours; and yours isn't mine; and ours wasn't Matt's; and Matt's wasn't ours. The common thread in each of our giving journeys is one word: *obedience.*

Are we willing to be obedient to what God has called us to? Are we willing to listen so that we can better grasp what He's calling us toward? Are we willing to ask ourselves, "How much is enough?" We know God doesn't need our money, but He graciously invites us to the incredible blessing of generosity—all to ultimately fulfill the Great Commission.

As I've counseled clients in this area, there are several thoughts and tools on giving that I have found to be extremely helpful and insightful, whether you're just beginning a journey of generosity or have been giving faithfully for many years.

First, we must be willing to start a giving journey if we have not yet begun to walk this path. Most of us have thought, *I can't afford to give now, but when I start making more money, or when I can get this debt paid off, or when I (fill in the blank), that's when I'll start giving.* The reality is that it becomes more challenging to give as your income and net worth increase. Starting where we are, right now, in our current situation, no matter how insignificant we believe the amount to be, giving is a step of obedience and faith to walk in alignment with God's plan for your life.

I shared this with my client Ethan during a recent financial planning meeting. As I sat down with him, I was honestly a little surprised Ethan wasn't already charitably giving. Though he was only in his late twenties, he was already a leader in his local church, teaching Bible studies, and mentoring young men to grow in their spiritual walks.

I gently asked, "Ethan, we always want to talk through charitable giving and discuss any goals you may have in this area. It doesn't look like you've begun a giving journey yet, and I would love to hear your thoughts."

Ethan stumbled and fumbled with his next words. "Bethany, I'm embarrassed about this. It just feels like I'm barely making ends meet, and I'm not doing anything irresponsible with my money. Anyway, whatever I could give would be nothing compared to what others are giving. My small amount wouldn't even matter."

I smiled encouragingly as he reluctantly glanced up and met my eyes. "Ethan, thank you for your willingness to share. I know this is a vulnerable subject, and I'm so grateful you know this is a safe place for us to grow together in a completely judgment-free zone. I would love to talk about this for a few minutes just to encourage you. Would that be okay?"

"Of course," Ethan said. "I'm here to learn."

I leaned across the desk as if I had an incredibly impactful secret to share. "Ethan, God has so much planned for you. His plan for you is good, and His path for you is a path He is uniquely equipping only you to walk. And part of that plan, as a believer, is giving. Not because God needs our money, but because God invites us to be part of what He's doing, and we grow through that journey."

This opened a door for us to continue discussing what the Bible says about giving. We began to talk through precepts and verses that are vital for every Christian to know as we seek to honor the Lord in our own giving journeys.

Precepts for Giving

Also found in Appendix B

1. Giving is a tangible way to acknowledge the ultimate ownership and provision of the sovereign God in our lives (see 1 Corinthians 4:7; Deuteronomy 8:16-18; Haggai 2:8; Psalms 24:1; 50:10-11).
2. We show honor and obedience to God in our giving. God commands us to give (see Proverbs 3:9-10; 1 Timothy 6:17-19; Luke 6:38).
3. Charitable giving is done in order to help prioritize the issues of life. Giving breaks the power of money (see Luke 16:11-13; Proverbs 18:10-11; Luke 12:33-34; 1 Timothy 6:9-10).
4. Charitable giving is done to meet the needs of others (see Exodus 16:18; 2 Corinthians 8:15; 9:12-14; Deuteronomy 15:10-11; Philippians 4:16; 1 John 3:17).
5. We draw personal rewards from the act of giving (see Revelation 22:12; 2 Corinthians 5:10; Matthew 6:20; Luke 12:33; Philippians 4:17; Matthew 16:27; 1 Corinthians 3:8-14).
6. Giving is an expression of worship and gratitude (see John 3:16; Romans 12:1; 2 Corinthians 8:1-6).

As Ethan mulled over these principles, he said, "So basically, I could start with anything?"

"Yes! Absolutely!" I chuckled and nodded. "As you gain clarity through this financial planning process we've been in together, these principles and scriptures will help guide you as you ask the Lord for some specifics on where He would have you begin. If you decide to give five dollars a week, that's a start! That's a step saying, 'Lord, I trust You. I trust You with my life, my money, and my everything.' And as a believer, once you experience the joy of giving, God will continue to work in you—not just the amount you're giving, though He desires for us to give cheerfully, regularly, and in proportion to what He's given us—and the ripple effects of generosity will flow into every area of your life. I can't wait to see what God does in this next year as you begin a whole new adventure!"

These are some of the most delightful conversations I have as a financial advisor. Furthering God's kingdom through giving is a privilege. Unlike Ethan, who was just starting his giving journey, many of us are already on that path, but we need some structure. Some tools. Some ideas to help us with organization, or tax efficiency, or even just simplicity. Here, I will share some ideas with you.

Create a Spontaneous-Giving Savings Bucket

If you're already consistently giving what you feel called to give but would like more room to bless others unexpectedly, creating a spontaneous-giving savings bucket can be a wonderful way to accomplish that goal. Many times, as women, we are more empathetic and attuned to needs around us.

For me, a spontaneous-giving bucket helps when I want to bless my kids' teachers with flowers and donuts.

Or if we desire to give a special offering to a mission trip for one of Landon's former students, the bucket makes that possible.

When I have a client who runs a nonprofit, and I feel led to make a gift to their ministry, I have the means to do that.

Or if my dear friend Alexis and her family have a need for one of their foster children, the spontaneous-giving bucket is there and waiting.

Funding even a small amount in a rhythm—like per paycheck—can be a fantastic way to grow this bucket. I know this sounds simple, but we need to know where our money is going, where we're spending our funds, and we don't want to take from funds earmarked for bills. (This was my problem, occasionally, before I began this giving bucket!) When we have a spontaneous-giving bucket to pull from, we are always ready and waiting for God to show us the next person He desires to bless through our obedience.

Consider Creating and Utilizing a Giving Grid

In the book *The Eternity Portfolio* by Alan Gotthardt, he introduces the concept of a giving grid and provides detailed instructions on thinking through and setting up this giving strategy.[1] The basic premise is praying about and deciding upon a base percentage to give on a certain amount of income or investments. For instance, if we make $100,000 this year, Landon and I have agreed to give 10 percent. That's the first stairstep on the grid. So on anything we receive up to $100,000, we will be tithing 10 percent, charitably. If the Lord chooses to bless us with a gift or a bonus or a commission, God has led us to give 15 percent on any funds between $100,000 and $150,000. Notice that the base percentage changes at a predetermined point. What we're going to give is decided *before* funds tangibly come into the picture.

In my family, we're sometimes living life on life's terms. We're surviving baseball practices, chorus concerts, work responsibilities, and so on, and there's little to no intentionality as we think about something like charitable giving. When we don't spend intentional time asking God what to do with money, it somehow disappears. We do what we always have done and keep on going—leaving no space to ask the Lord, "I know You see my whole picture. Will You help me map out what would be obedient and sacrificial—what You desire for me and my life as I seek to steward my everything for You?" When we do this, I guarantee that God will show up.

Open a Donor-Advised Fund (DAF)

A donor-advised fund (DAF) is a charitable investment account for the purpose of supporting the organizations close to your heart. In my experience, DAFs are the fastest-growing charitable giving vehicle in the United States because they are one of the easiest and most tax-advantageous ways to give to charity. When you contribute cash, securities, or other assets to a DAF, you are generally eligible to take an immediate tax deduction. You can then invest those funds for tax-free growth, and you can recommend grants to any eligible IRS-qualified public charity.

And an important note: Once a donor (the person charitably giving the funds) moves money into a DAF, the donor no longer has full control of the funds, and the DAF could disallow certain contributions. Therefore, the doctrine, philosophy, and governing documents of the DAF you choose are important. Many believers have benefited from selecting a Christian DAF.

Give Appreciated Assets

Assets in your investment accounts tend to go up in value over time. Normally, if you sell investments in a taxable investment account that have experienced growth, you must realize those gains and pay what's called a capital gains tax. Did you know that you have the option of giving those appreciated assets to charity? In doing this, you avoid having to pay the capital gains tax and the charity does not have to pay it either, because they're a tax-exempt organization. A win-win!

You can then keep the cash you would have given for living expenses.

You can reinvest the cash in the investment account.

You can even give the appreciated assets and keep the cash for your spontaneous-giving bucket.

If this sounds like a confusing concept, I can see why. Don't forget there are like-minded advisors who specialize in areas just like this to help you give more to the kingdom.

Bundle Charitable Giving

When we pay our taxes, we have the opportunity to take advantage of some deductions that help benefit us when calculating our tax liability. We add up things like mortgage interest, charitable giving, state and local taxes, and more. We are able to take those dollar amounts as a tax deduction.

Depending on the amount of these deductions each year, we either itemize them, or we take the standard deduction if it's higher. In the past, the standard deduction was pretty low, and my family always itemized because the addition of the listed expenses was more than the amount of the standard deduction. But, in recent years, the standard deduction has increased so much that many of us, even if we are generous givers, take the standard deduction rather than itemizing.

The basic idea of bundling giving is that you double up giving in one year (itemize that year) and then take the standard deduction in the second year. While giving is a priority whether there's a tax advantage or not, it can be advantageous to think through giving strategies in these seasons when the standard deduction is so high.

As you read through the ideas above, some may seem easy to implement, while others may seem daunting and a bit more complicated. The important thing is to start somewhere, be an equal contributor to giving discussions with your spouse if you are married, and if you need guidance, don't hesitate to ask a trusted source for help. Take one step, and God will meet you where you are.

And God did just that as I had the privilege of watching Him work on our family's generosity several Christmases ago.

I jerked our gray Honda Odyssey sharply to the left as Silas pointed and yelled, "That lady, Mom. It's that lady God's telling me to give my money to."

I don't normally drive erratically in our hometown traffic while passing out cash. But this was a different Christmas season. A Christmas season with a new tradition.

Several weeks before this unusual detour during our Saturday errands, I'd learned of our Blue Trust Holiday Giving Challenge. As our national managing director shared his heart and the details of this challenge in a short video, my interest was immediately piqued. As many of us tithe and charitably give online in this age of technology, our transactional giving methods have the potential to suck the inspiration and joy out of the process. And clicking buttons online to make a donation has made it more difficult to light a fire of generosity under our children's feet as they grow and begin learning how to handle money.

The instructions of the challenge were this:

Go to our children (or nieces, nephews, grandchildren, dear friends' children—be creative!) and give them some amount of money they could then use to practice generosity. It could be $25; it could be $1,000. The amount didn't matter, but what did matter was the autonomy our children were to have in the choice of who or where to give these funds. The children had the power to choose—completely on their own (and with no judgment from us as adults)—how they would bless others through generosity.

For James and Silas, this was an interesting conversation.

"So, wait a minute," said James, 11 years old at the time. "You're saying you're going to give me a lot of money—50 whole dollars—and I get to choose what to do with it. But I can't keep it. I can't save it for the new Nintendo Switch? I need to give it away to someone else or to an organization that helps people?"

My face lit up as I heard him repeat the instructions I'd just shared. "Yes! You've got it, Buddy!"

Landon and I handed out two twenties and two fives to both of our boys. Not just a fifty, in case they wanted to split up the money.

In typical fashion, James held on to his for a few weeks, thoughtfully considering his options.

Also in typical fashion, Silas quickly decided what to do with his cash.

And this is how we arrived at the Saturday before Christmas, when I jerked the family van hard to the left, into a gas station parking lot where a woman walked through, looking defeated and worn down.

Though I pulled into the parking lot somewhat abruptly, I tried to pull up beside the dear woman without her thinking we were attempting to run her over. As we slowed to place the van in park, I turned and said to Silas, "Babe, this is your money that you feel God has told you to give to this woman. I want you to tell her. I'm going to roll your window down, and you share anything with her you want."

He shrugged and said, "Okay, Mom. I'm going to give her 25 dollars and keep my other half to give to someone else."

This precious soul seemed genuinely shocked when we pulled up beside her, the passenger backseat van window rolled down with Silas sticking his head out and waving his bills at her.

She stared at us, unsure of our reason for this bizarre stop.

Silas proceeded to say, in his sweetest six-year-old voice, "Excuse me, ma'am. I want to give you this. It's a present for you. God loves you."

And that's all he said.

I could see her eyes fill with tears as her hand gently took the cash from Silas. I don't remember her next words, but I do remember her eyes.

What her eyes conveyed in that moment, no words could have expressed. Her eyes seemed to say, "I am seen. I am someone. I am valued."

And I immediately thought of two special verses in the Bible.

Hagar, when on the run and suffering relational turmoil, was comforted by the angel of the Lord. In response, "She gave this name to the LORD who spoke to her: 'You are the God who sees me,' for she said, 'I have now seen the One who sees me'" (Genesis 16:13).

Also, Jesus tells us, "If you give even a cup of cold water to one of the least of my followers, you will surely be rewarded" (Matthew 10:42 NLT).

It was only 25 dollars. But the very evident takeaway was that it wasn't about the money. It was about the act itself. The care that was conveyed in the gesture. As we drove away, Silas's face gleamed with joy. While he never watches me as I click the series of buttons to tithe when our paychecks are deposited into our checking accounts each month, this simple act of him—by himself—being his own boss to choose what to do with money to bless someone taught a lesson worth far more than 50 dollars.

Silas saved his remaining cash to make Christmas gift bags for a few folks who lived in a lower-income housing area of our town. We purchased cute bags and placed bottled waters, snacks, and a devotional in each, and then delivered those bags to doorsteps.

James took a bit longer to decide how to give his money away, which was no surprise to us. Christmas was fast approaching, and I'd reminded him twice about the money. I'd offered suggestions of organizations to which he could donate. He would nod his head and thoughtfully say, "Okay, Mom. I'm still thinking about it."

Christmas was on a Saturday that year, and as we headed to visit our families in Florida on Christmas Eve, we stopped for lunch at our usual exit—the Taylor Road exit in Montgomery, Alabama. This exit has several pros and one con. The pros are that the restaurants are close to the interstate, and there are countless restaurant choices—a Chick-fil-A and a Starbucks sit side by side (and I'm pretty sure that's how it will be in heaven). There is only one con. Major traffic. Major, major, *major* traffic. People everywhere. Long drive-through lines. Long restroom lines.

James still had not spent his money, but unbeknownst to me, he had been carrying it in his pocket, every day, everywhere he went.

As we turned right out of Chick-fil-A onto the busy thoroughfare and waited at yet another light, a gentleman holding a cardboard sign stood at the corner by a light pole. He had several disposable grocery bags at his feet, which appeared to hold all his worldly possessions. I was focused on giving each person in our family the correct food, and Landon was focused on not getting in an accident as he watched the traffic around us and was stopped near the back of a long line of cars waiting for the light to turn green. All of a sudden, James yelled, "Unlock my door! I need to give my money to that man!" At what felt like the speed of light, Landon unlocked his door, and I yelled, "Hurry, the light is about to change!"

We watched from the front seat of the van as James ran to the man and handed him the 50 dollars. James's face shone as he ran back and jumped into his passenger seat. He'd taken a good while longer than Silas when deciding where to give his money, but when he knew, he knew.

It's been said that generosity is the antidote to materialism.

And in this Nintendo Switch, PlayStation, Xbox, expensive-toys-for-kids world, we must be intentional to instill generosity into our children. They will not magically become generous people when they become adults. Even if I explain to them, "Listen, I know you never saw us tithe, but I promise we did. We just did it online, and I always faithfully pushed the button each week." So what? That will move the needle by zero degrees.

The world is telling our children to spend and buy and keep on buying. The Bible is telling us to practice being generous because the Lord was first generous to us. That first year of the generosity Christmas challenge was special, as it reminded me of God's individual and unique wiring in each of my boys. And whether you have children of your own, nephews, nieces, or grandchildren to love, or simply friends' children who are in your orbit of life, I encourage you to try this experiment and sit back to watch what happens. What you've probably already figured out is that you will be far more blessed than they will be as you have a front-row seat to view the kingdom of God coming alive—on earth as in heaven—just as Jesus intended.

Several times a week, I pray a variation of the following verse for my clients: "Whether you turn to the right or to the left, your ears will hear a voice behind you, saying, 'This is the way; walk in it'" (Isaiah 30:21).

And I find the paraphrase of this passage in *The Message* fascinating, especially when continuing to verse 22: "Your teacher will be right there, local and on the job, urging you on whenever you wander left or right: 'This is the right road. Walk down this road.' You'll scrap your expensive and fashionable god-images. You'll throw them in the trash as so much garbage, saying, 'Good riddance!'" (Isaiah 30:21-22).

Friend, this is *it*. This is life, indeed. This is stewarding our everything. You can do this. Is it scary? Sure! Do we need our money in order to actually pay our bills and live? Absolutely! But does the Father want to do more in our lives than we could ask or imagine? One hundred percent. And He sees the whole picture, more than we ever could. His heart breaks as He urges us with immense love to scrap our expensive and fashionable god-images, and instead to trust Him.

Remember Matt and the $40,000 he gave us? Guess what? That's not your journey. And it's not mine. It was part of Matt's giving journey, and we were fortunate enough to be blessed by it. Each of our own giving journeys is just as amazing. Just as distinctive. Just as unique. Just as full of seemingly impossible possibilities.

When God formed you in your mother's womb, He created you with plans to prosper you and not harm you, to give you hope and a future (Jeremiah 29:11). And that hope includes generosity. That life includes obedience in giving. That future includes giving your life away.

Who knows? One day you may slide onto a Whataburger bench and find yourself following God's leading in a way you couldn't have fathomed.

6

You Lead the Way

Teaching Kids to Steward God's Resources Well

"I'm just confused. My brain is not working right. I need to choose another brain," declared three-year-old Silas at one o'clock in the morning as he clutched my hand in the hospital parking lot.

Earlier, in the hours leading up to Silas's brain not working right, all seemed at peace with the world. Our family had been apart for a week, and we were delighted to be reunited. Landon had been attending a counseling conference, I was at a work conference, and the boys were in Florida with grandparents attending Grammie and Gator-Pa's summer Vacation Bible School at their church. We were thankful to be back together and exhausted from the respective week we had each experienced. Bedtime came quickly, and after putting both boys to bed, Landon and I collapsed on the couch. This was only after Silas tried to sneak into our room right after I put him to bed, and when I reprimanded him, he said, "But I cannot exist without you." Alas, I should have kept him with me and just coexisted, which might have avoided the excitement that was to come. But instead, I sent him back to bed. And just as Landon and I flopped on the couch to eat a little chocolate ice cream and watch a TV show together…

I heard choking. Big choking. And instead of immediately becoming concerned, I knew what was happening, and it made me mad. I did hurry into Silas's room, but I knew he had coins in his hand when he went to bed, and I figured. I just knew by my mommy senses he had put a penny in his mouth and choked on it. Recent to this episode, Silas had begun to love holding coins in his hands. He was learning to count pennies. As I entered his room, he was crying, but he was able to stop choking, and then he yelled, "I SWALLOWED DAT PENNY!" In a panic, I left Landon with him and went to our room to hurriedly change out of my pajamas into regular clothes to go to the emergency room.

Now, I know, I know, in some cases you don't *need* to take your kid to the ER when he swallows something that's not food. But I do because, for me, it's better to be safe than sorry. So regardless of his health, for my own peace of mind, I had to take him.

Silas came in my room and told me he had his Crocs on and was ready to go to the emergency room. We arrived at the ER and filled out a sticker with Silas's info. Right at the top the sticker read, "Reason for visit."

I wrote, "Ate a penny."

Hospital staff called us into triage, and I explained the penny situation. "Did you watch him eat it?" they asked. I said, "No, but I might as well have. He's very articulate," I told them, "and if he says he ate the penny, he ate it." They let me know they would take an x-ray of his stomach and then the doctor would meet with us to look at it.

Back in the waiting room, I was in a constant state of the willies. Every part of me felt the very definition of the nonofficial term meaning "a feeling of nervousness, fear, or creepiness." One patient had been in a fight, and his face was all kinds of bruised and bloody. We sat across the room, away from most people, but I happened to sit by the only trash can in the area, and the man from the fight kept coming over to throw away bloody tissues and his empty Reese's wrappers. One lady was moaning constantly (and it wasn't me, I promise). It was a sad situation, but it was the emergency room, so what else should I have expected?

We waited. Thankfully, the x-ray technician came to get us from the waiting room, and we followed her to have the images taken. Silas was as still as a statue. And that was when things took a turn for the interesting. After taking a couple of scans, she walked out from behind the special radiation protection wall and said, "We don't see a penny."

Um, no. No, you just didn't say that. I said, "Well, he's very articulate, and if he says he swallowed a penny, he definitely swallowed a penny. I heard him choking and trying to figure out if he should swallow it or keep choking." The tech said, "Okay then, let me take another couple of x-rays from the top of his head through his entire torso." So Silas held on to a handlebar and performed like a champ. We reconvened in the adjacent room, and the technician showed Silas and me the x-rays. I said, "Silas, look at your whole skeleton!" He said, "I don't like my skeleton, and I wish I didn't have a skeleton." It was a bit creepy, and it looked like he really had too many teeth. Way too many.

The x-ray tech said, "Do you see how my sticker shows up on here—showing this is his left side? That's because it's copper. It sticks out on the x-ray—big time. That's what that penny should be doing. There's no penny in his body. But of course, I'll send this to the radiologist now and let him look at it, and then the doctor will meet with you."

Back to the waiting room with our new best friends we went. But not before we visited the emergency room public bathroom, and Silas took a drink from the water fountain. It was almost too much for this sanitizer-carrying, germophobic mom to handle. And then we waited. And we waited. And we still waited. Silas danced on the coffee table benches. We played pretend games. We watched *Ralph Breaks the Internet* on my phone.

Finally. The moment of reckoning. It was now around 11:45 p.m. We were called back. The doctor said, "When the radiologist said in his report that there was no penny, I didn't believe it. I pulled it up myself to check. But, Mom, there's absolutely no penny. He didn't swallow a penny." And poor Silas, he was so confused. I could see he was upset because he truly, sincerely thought he did. And so did I. The doctor looked in his throat, and it looked great. She looked in his ears…just to check them…upon which Silas informed her that he *swallowed* the penny, and it wasn't in his ears. He also let her know that by now the penny must be down in his leg, so why were we looking in his tummy? The doctor gave a short lecture on the importance of only putting food into our mouths, and then we waited for our discharge papers.

After some time, we were brought the papers. Silas was so tired, and I was tired. In my mind, I was already formulating the email to my boss to let him know I needed to come in a little later on Monday morning.

Hand in hand, we walked out of the automatic doors. As we walked, Silas, in his sweet little spunky voice said, "Mom, maybe I spit out dat penny." And, with probably $1,300 down the tubes (since we'd barely begun working on our deductible for the year), I just smiled, felt sorry for him, and said, "It's okay, Bud." As I buckled him into his seat, he said, "I'm just confused. My brain is not working right. I need to choose another brain." And with that, we drove home, took baths because we'd been in an emergency room, and quickly fell asleep.

This story makes it very clear that counting coins trumps swallowing coins every single time. As my boys have grown through different ages and stages, Landon and I have handled money differently with them in each season. These real-life experiences have helped me guide my clients as we discuss how to raise money-smart children—whether that's your own children, grandkids, nieces and nephews, or children in your sphere of influence. As adults, we desire to help children become godly, productive, and effective members of society. In my work, I have found that the more financial wealth an individual has, the tougher it is to teach children the principles they need to learn to be wise with money as they get older.

In contrast to material possessions and certain skills, we know that character and values cannot be given or purchased. As Tim Kimmel says, "You can't leave character in a trust account. You cannot write your values into the will. You cannot bank traits like courage, honesty, and compassion in a safe deposit box. What we need is a plan—a long-term strategy to convey our convictions and good money management skills to the next generation."[1]

What do we desire to teach the children who are under our care? Are our current spending decisions—from buying their clothes to funding their education—furthering our desires? As we provide for our own children or the children within our sphere, let's consider giving them more than just money, possessions, and opportunities. Let's commit to leaving them with a legacy of character and wisdom that can be passed down from generation to generation.

Raising Money-Smart Kids

Financial literacy starts at home. In 2022, only 23 states in the US required a personal finance class for high school graduation, placing the burden of financial education primarily on parents.[2] While the number of states where this class is required is, thankfully, on the rise, we are still many years away from a time when all schools will be offering this type of education for their students.

Children can begin to manage money at a very early age and have the ability to make independent money decisions at ages four or five. By the time they reach ages eight or nine, if they are properly trained, they may be responsible enough to plan for and buy items they want or need. There are numerous methods to teach children good money management and decision-making skills. As adults, we can relay stories of how we have earned, saved, and spent money at different stages during our lives. We can also fill their minds with lessons on the importance of being careful and wise with money. However, the best way for them to learn is through experience—managing money and making decisions themselves. Our goal should not be to tell our children "yes" or "no" regarding financial decisions but to become a consultant and provide wisdom as they weigh whether a spending decision is worth the cost.

Where and how we spend money is largely a function of where and how our parents spent money. The same can be said for our children. We do not have to say a thing to our children for them to know our priorities, commitments, and habits. After seeing behavior modeled, children will either emulate that behavior or react to it and behave in the opposite way. If children are going to become financially responsible, then wise money management must be consistently modeled and instilled in them over the long term.

Around the time Silas thought he swallowed a penny, I realized we had a thief in our home. As you may have guessed, his name was Silas, and at the time, we allowed this to continue for a little while because he was a very sweet thief. He would scramble around looking for money that we had set down on a counter or placed in a drawer. He called loose change "coins" and he called dollar bills "big dollars."

After his thieving had gone on for some time, and even though we don't use this phrase at home, Silas began to say, "I'm rich! I am so rich since I have big dollars."

I don't really like the sentence, "I'm rich," when referring to big dollars. In my life and during my interactions with families and individuals throughout the years, I have seen time and time again that "big dollars" don't make someone rich. As I'm sure we've all experienced, there are a whole bunch of people who have a whole bunch of big dollars who are very unhappy.

So this was the time I began to try to shape the I'm-rich mindset for my children. I tried several times to explain that we can be rich in *many* areas of our lives—not only in big dollars.

We can be rich in Jesus Christ.

We can be rich in love.

We can be rich in family.

We can be rich in friends.

We can be rich in fellowship—just hanging out together and spending quality time.

Silas seemed to comprehend this concept. Sort of.

A couple nights after my oh-so eloquent explanation of the word *rich*, we were in the midst of Silas's bedtime ritual, and I asked him what he was hoping to receive for Christmas. First, he let me know he was going to ask for a car he could drive when he became an adult. I told him that was a great idea (I try not to discourage creativity and dreaming big), however, if he did receive a car, and the car sat for ten years until he was able to drive it, the car wouldn't work anymore. Cars can't just sit for a long time. So I encouraged him to wait on the vehicle wish.

Processing this, he thought for a minute more and then said, "I am asking for a new door."

What?

"A new door?" I asked. "Like, for our house, or for your room, or what?"

"For my room," he said. "You know how we can be rich in things besides big dollars—I would like to be rich in doors. I am asking for a gold door for my bedroom for Christmas. You know, rich in doors."

Who thinks this kind of thing? And even if someone *did* think of odd ways to be "rich," how would one even come to the idea of a gold door for his bedroom? I am continually astonished by Silas's creativity.

Over the years, I have thought of this story many times when dwelling on how impressionable children are and how they are watching every move we make far more than they are listening to the words we say. This influence is why it's vital for us to examine our own lives as we seek to teach our children about money.

Start by Examining Yourself

Developing a training plan for our children starts with us. Here are some questions to help us determine if we want to pass on our personal money management principles to our children. Before we begin training our children, we want to ensure our own house is in order.

1. Do I have financial goals for the next year, next five years, and beyond?
2. Do I have a spending plan for the next 12 months?
3. Do I know the amount of debt I have? Do I have a plan to pay off my debt?
4. What would happen to my family financially if I lost my job or income?
5. Am I giving charitably on a regular basis?
6. Do I spend impulsively?
7. What does my lifestyle communicate regarding my value system?
8. Am I saving and investing for the future?
9. If married, in what areas do my spouse and I disagree about money? How do we work those disagreements out?
10. If someone did not know me and had access to my

checking account for the last five years, what story could be written about my life?

- What do I prioritize?
- What are my habits?
- Am I satisfied with my relationship with the Lord?
- For what do I choose to take on debt?
- Can I afford where I've chosen to live?

Take a deep breath. Come on, let's take a deep breath together. I think we need it. Whew, that was quite a list of questions, and I felt some shame creeping into my own mind and heart as I read through one or two of them. I encourage you to think of these challenging questions, not as an indictment, but as an invitation. An invitation to take a step in a wise financial direction. An invitation to move toward all God has for us as women of worth. I promise you and I aren't the only ones to struggle in some of these areas. Remember, it's never too late to take one step. And then another. And then another. Convicting questions are tough sometimes, but they can help us recognize the truth, surrender our own will to Jesus, and lean on Him to show us the way. Thank goodness we don't have to be perfect to teach our children how to wisely handle money. But we do need to be sincerely working in each of these areas above, and we need to be honest with our kids.

Many of us may have grown up in households where money conversations were taboo. It may have been obvious that mom and dad weren't on the same page about money, and because their communication surrounding money was broken, we learned early on not to ask questions about money. The message may have been, "Money is private (or bad), and we don't talk about it."

Or maybe you grew up in a home where money was talked about. Where giving was transparent and big decisions were discussed openly. If this is you, what a blessing! In my home growing up, the checkbook sat on the end table between two couches, and Mom or Dad picked it up often to record purchases. They talked openly about our grocery budget and discussed upcoming expenses in front of my sister and me. They exercised wisdom, knowing our ages and maturity levels, as they chose how much information to share and when. They allowed us to learn from them without placing the burden of adult financial management on our shoulders.

Thus, in our home with James and Silas, Landon and I have tried to maintain an open posture around finances. A mindset of: There's nothing you can't ask us. And we ask the Lord to give us wisdom as we answer our kids' questions in an age-appropriate fashion. However, I learned something very valuable in the last couple of years as James has grown up to be a teenager.

You'll recall James is our eldest child, and he's a by-the-book rule follower. He worries about others and is sensitive to shifts and changes in the emotions of those around him. He's a perfectionist and very hard on himself when he doesn't live up to his own (sometimes unrealistic) expectations. Recently, we took a trip to the Orlando area to visit family and sightsee. One morning as we readied ourselves for a day of fun, Silas appeared in the doorway.

"Mom," he said, "James broke my glasses."

"Oh, no," I responded, "I'm sure they're not broken. Let me take a look."

I knelt down to gently take the glasses from him, and sure enough, one of the arms was broken off.

"How did this happen?" I asked.

"It was just an accident." Silas said. "James and I were wrestling, and his hand accidentally hit my glasses on the side, and they broke."

I considered what to do next. Silas began wearing glasses at two years old, and until a few months before this, he'd worn glasses that were nearly indestructible with a strap that wrapped around his head, connecting the two arms of the glasses. But because he was now in fourth grade, we encouraged him to let the strap-glasses go and give some big-boy glasses a try. These were the big-boy glasses in the palm of my hand, with one arm missing.

As I continued to talk to Silas about a plan of action, I could hear Landon in the next room consoling James. He was very upset that Silas's glasses were broken, and he blamed himself for it. Because James was almost six feet tall, and the boys are five years apart, there's a huge difference between them in both size and strength. James knows this, and we've talked—time and time again—about him not using all his strength when he plays with Silas. The conversation I was overhearing was going smoothly with an appropriate balance of compassion and brotherly guilt until my ears and heart were pricked as I heard James say, "And Dad, I know we're on this vacation, and I know it's costing us $3,000 to be here this week and to do all of this. We can't afford to replace Silas's glasses. We don't have the money." At this point, I heard James begin to cry.

I was reminded in that moment, while it's a huge win to be transparent to your kids about money, allowing them to see how you handle money responsibly, it's just as important to make sure they know the weight of the world is not on their shoulders and they are not responsible for the family's finances. James was just a 14-year-old kid. Landon quickly jumped in and said, "Buddy, it's not your responsibility to pay for Silas's glasses. We have eye insurance and an emergency fund for unexpected things that happen—expenses you don't plan for. It's our job, as your parents, to plan well for times like this, and while we're sorry this happened and hope you will recognize your own strength more clearly next time, we're just glad Silas wasn't hurt, and we're prepared to handle the expense of new glasses."

Now, let me be clear. If James continued to wrestle with Silas, and Silas's glasses were repeatedly broken after every impromptu match, that would be a different conversation in the future. Then, it might be helpful for James to have some "skin in the game" and pay for a portion of the glasses. But that wasn't the case that day.

My point is that all children are wired differently—just like all adults are wired differently. It's important and extremely helpful to be transparent regarding money, in an age-appropriate way, with our kids. It's also important for them to know they aren't responsible for the family finances. And it is critical for us as the adults in their lives to know their personalities and dispositions in order to thoughtfully tailor our conversations with them for their benefit and understanding.

Guiding Principles When Teaching Kids About Money

Effective financial training requires commitment, patience, and faith. It's a long-term process involving time, effort, and sometimes money. Approach it prayerfully, model the principles for your children, and let them practice, even fail, in a safe environment. Skills are strengthened through repeated practice. Consider these five teaching principles as you think about pouring into your children in the area of money:

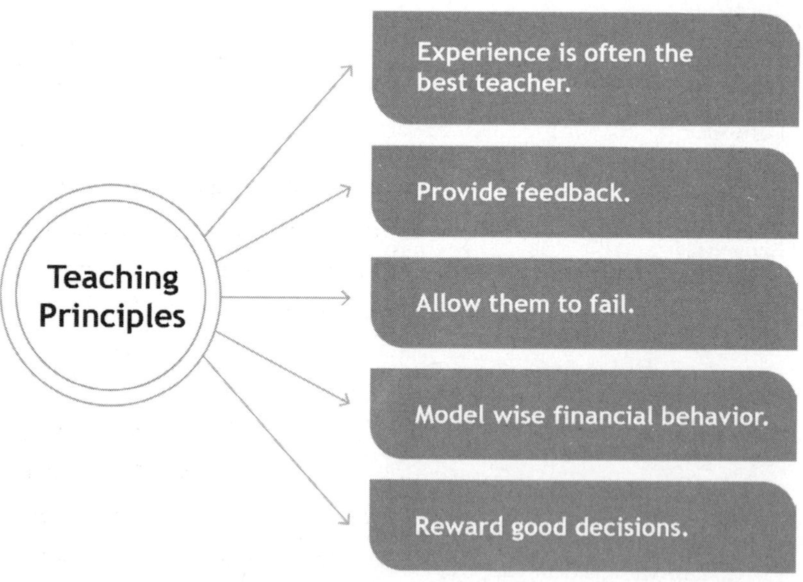

Experience Is Often the Best Teacher

The most effective way to learn is through experience. While we can tell children about money, it only becomes meaningful when they experience the joy of giving, the reward of saving, and the satisfaction of spending wisely. Provide opportunities for hands-on practice. For example, allowing older children to borrow money and repay that debt under parental supervision can be a powerful learning experience.

Provide Feedback

Children need the opportunity to make choices within clearly defined boundaries. As parents, it's important to decide in advance what values we want to teach them—morally, socially, financially, and spiritually. When providing feedback, parents should use the opportunity to discuss, guide, and teach without belittling or punishing them. Praise their successes and offer encouragement, and if (or should I say *when*) they make mistakes, calmly explore alternative choices and how those choices may have impacted the outcome.

Allow Them to Fail

Mistakes and frustration are part of life. The issue is not whether children will fail but how they will respond when they do. Teaching them how to come back after failure and disappointment is the goal—not perfection. Failure should be treated as a positive learning experience because it teaches you how to overcome challenges and persevere. The best time for kids to fail is when they are young and parents are available to walk alongside them through those hurdles.

Model Wise Financial Behavior

I sometimes quote Roz, the undercover desk clerk from the movie *Monsters, Inc.* to my kids. You know the line—the one about always watching. Can't you just hear her saying it? This quote reminds me that our kids are always watching us. They take note of what we do, what we say, and what we prioritize. It's important to model consistent, wise money management so that they can learn by example. One idea could be to involve your children in the grocery shopping process and explain how to compare prices, quality, and brands. The grocery store is a fantastic learning environment to practice comparisons between generic versus brand-name items or sale versus non-sale items. Or you might decide to start making your coffee at home instead of running through Starbucks every morning for that venti vanilla latte. Lifestyle and routine changes like this are prime opportunities to share our decision-making processes with our children. We don't want to waste even small decisions we make to steward our funds wisely, allowing our children to learn from those decisions.

Reward Good Decisions

Rewards are motivational and provide another source of feedback and incentive for all of us, but especially children. Reinforcements can come in many forms, including treats, activities, verbal praise, money, etc. When children are rewarded for good decision-making, they feel competent and encouraged to continue making wise choices.

My friend's daughter recently traveled to a camp in southern Georgia for an entire week away. Her older sister had attended the same camp during several previous summers, but this was the younger sister's very first time to attend as a big girl—eight years old! Before my friend and her husband left her for the week, they stopped by the canteen shop to let their sweet girl pick out a treat. She had her own spending money for camp, but mom and dad letting her pick out a treat on drop-off day was a special tradition she remembered her big sister also enjoying in previous years. The air was cold and refreshing in the shop and smelled like sweaty kids. My friend showed her daughter a camp T-shirt, but that wasn't what she wanted. Next, mom offered a sticker for her water bottle—a sticker just like her big sister had—but she turned that down as well. Finally, the big-girl camper decisively walked over to a little paddle with a ball and string attached to it and a pink, beaded plastic bracelet that appeared it might break if you looked at it too intently. Her parents knew these were not wise purchases and warned her that they would break easily, and most likely, wouldn't last a day at camp. Their daughter agreed, and sadly, they left without making a purchase.

At the end of the week, mom and dad excitedly drove into the parking lot to pick up their little camper. They each bent down to scoop her up in huge bear hugs and couldn't wait to hear about every detail of camp life. Their sweet daughter chattered on about this and that, and eventually, mom and dad asked how she'd spent her spending money at the canteen. She blushed and looked down, embarrassed as she whispered, "I bought a Snickers bar." Her parents looked at each other with confusion. Why had she only chosen a candy bar? She had enough money to buy more than only one candy bar.

It was true she had money to buy more, but she didn't feel confident or empowered to make a spending decision that would please her parents (or that she would not get in trouble for), so she chose something she knew was acceptable in their eyes.

On one hand, we could look at this as a lesson in wise spending decisions. On the other hand, this could have been a prime opportunity to let a child fail when the stakes were very low. So what if she bought the $1 plastic bracelet? She probably would have enjoyed it for a few days, and then it would have broken. But she would have felt the empowerment of making her very own spending decision with joy and confidence. And, best of all, she would have learned all on her very own that she might not choose that same $1 bracelet again.

Goodness, it is hard to give up control. As a recovering helicopter parent, trust me, I know! It's tough to watch our children fail. Kids are not always going to make the right (or even the best) choices, and that's part of growing up. They are at the beginning of the Lord orchestrating their individual stories, and thankfully, their stories include formative years when we have the privilege of walking alongside our children—or other children under our care—to lead, guide, and support them when $1 pink beaded bracelets fall apart.

Raising children is not for the faint of heart. But the rewards far outweigh the challenges. God has given us these precious souls to shepherd and pour into, and this holy responsibility also includes allowing them to spread their wings and learn to steward their everything for Jesus.

Developing Perspective

Our beliefs and perspective toward money management affects our decision-making and behavior. It has great potential for good or for harm in our lives. Teaching children the right perspective and understanding of money is a critical part of preparing them for their future.

Children will have lots of questions about money. Whose money is it? What is money for? How do you earn money? One of the best things we can do is to educate them on what money is all about, where it comes from, what it is, and what it is not.

Money is all about stewardship. Stewardship is the use of God-given resources for the accomplishment of God-given goals. However, instead of stewardship, most people's perspective toward money is ownership. How you answer the question of "Whose money is it?" will ultimately determine how the money is used. Consider the following comparison on the two perspectives toward money:

Ownership	Stewardship
Has a tight hold on "my" money.	Understands that all money is from God.
Fears losing money or not having enough.	Has peace knowing that God will provide for all our needs.
Fears not knowing how best to use the money and the temptation to use it in a way that is not wise.	Has freedom knowing that God has a specific plan of how to use the resources He has entrusted to us.
Wrongly keeps a short-term perspective.	Understands that we will be held accountable for how we steward the money we have.

Along with a stewardship mindset, there are five key financial lessons all kids should know.

- Money has value and should be treated as valuable (see Proverbs 13:11).
- Money is earned through hard and continuous work (see Colossians 3:23).
- We are merely stewards of our wealth. God is the owner (see Psalm 24:1).
- Borrowing money is a slippery slope (see 1 Timothy 6:9-10).
- Be generous (see Luke 12:33-34).

Also, practical resources are always helpful when discussing a biblical money-management perspective and healthy habits and behaviors. At the back of this book, in appendices C, D, and E, are three different checklists that can be extremely beneficial to help guide you as you seek to pour wisdom into your children in the area of finances. Each checklist is tailored to a specific age group and offers practical exercises and practices you can implement with your kids.

Proverbs 22:6 tells us, "Train up a child in the way he should go, and when he is old he will not depart from it" (NKJV). As a mother, aunt, grandmother, close family friend, or mentor, it is your privilege to have a key role in shaping young, moldable hearts. It's too important a responsibility to ignore. Be encouraged, you're not in it alone! Take advantage of resources like God's Word, this book, and a community of believers around you. While I'm thankful that no one in my house is swallowing coins, the stakes are still high as James and Silas count their change and "big dollars" and continue to learn to be stewards of all God has entrusted to them. I'm cheering you on as you passionately pursue Jesus in this area!

7

You Are Called

How God Works Through Purposeful Goals

At the kitchen table during spring break a few years back, I plopped down in a chair next to my parents—right between them, of course—all three of us in our pajamas with steaming mugs of coffee warming our hands. As I pulled up Blue Trust's financial planning software, we discussed some impromptu financial matters that had come up in conversation. I usually don't show up to client meetings in snowman pajama pants, but hey, if the situation warrants pajamas, I always desire to be appropriately dressed.

Almost a year to the day before our pajama-breakfast gathering, my dad sold our family business—the John Deere and Kubota tractor dealership in my hometown. For a total of 47 years in the retail business, Dad faithfully rolled out of bed to head to work each day—not only to sell tractors, but to be salt and light for the kingdom as a Christian businessman.

He sold the business and retired just in time for him and my mom to begin traveling to central Florida every two weeks to help care for my grandmother, who was in her early nineties and struggling with Alzheimer's. God's timing was perfect.

Even before the sale of the business, my parents had begun to graciously allow me and Blue Trust to step in and guide them in their financial decisions. As a little girl, I watched my parents faithfully tithe in a rhythm every Sunday morning—placing a white printed envelope inside Dad's worn leather Bible before leaving home and dropping it in the offering plate. Mom and Dad had been appropriately open about their finances all along, so it seemed like a natural transition for me to begin helping as their financial advisor when the time came.

My parents desired to charitably give on the profits from the sale of the business, but they weren't exactly sure what churches, organizations, or charities to choose. So we opened a donor-advised fund, which enabled my parents to receive a charitable giving tax benefit the year the business was sold.

And that's what led us to the kitchen table that particular spring-break morning. My parents expressed their excitement and readiness to take action in sending money to the organizations to which they prayerfully felt led to give. It's one thing to watch someone write a weekly tithe check. It's an entirely different thing to watch someone gift dollar amounts with significant zeros at the end. The snowmen on my pajama pants danced while I clicked the keys on my laptop, and my parents looked on as we granted money to special places in their hearts.

The joy sacrificial giving can bring in our lives as Jesus followers can only be accomplished if we answer the question, "How much is enough?" My parents couldn't have wisely gifted their funds had we not worked together to fully understand their financial picture. Have you ever thought about this question? Honestly, if I begin to roll it around in my mind, my brain immediately goes into defensive mode, swirling into panic asking, "Why?" or "What if?" Why is it important to know how much is enough? I don't have a problem with debt, and I live on what I earn.

Why should I figure out something that feels ambiguous and so far in the future?

What if there are unanticipated job changes that negatively affect my financial situation?

What if someone in my family has a severe health problem and needs significant medical care?

What if I simply want to build bigger barns because that feels safer?

Let's face it, having money feels safe. You're not alone if you find security in a substantial savings account balance. For me, "what ifs" seem far less "what iffy" when I know there's a cushion to fall back on, and the larger the better.

I truly believe what Jesus says in Matthew 6:26-33,

> Look at the birds of the air; they do not sow or reap or store away in barns, and yet your heavenly Father feeds them. Are you not much more valuable than they? Can any one of you by worrying add a single hour to your life?
>
> And why do you worry about clothes? See how the flowers of the field grow. They do not labor or spin. Yet I tell you that not even Solomon in all his splendor was dressed like one of these. If that is how God clothes the grass of the field, which is here today and tomorrow is thrown into the fire, will he not much more clothe you—you of little faith? So do not worry, saying, "What shall we eat?" or "What shall we drink?" or "What shall we wear?" For the pagans run after all these things, and your heavenly Father knows that you need them. But seek first his kingdom and his righteousness, and all these things will be given to you as well.

If I say I'm on board with the verses above, why is it so hard to live them out? Why is it such a challenge to have a desire to figure out how much is enough? Why is it important to know, and then how is it possible to keep living out a lifestyle I've chosen based on my answer, day by day?

"How much is enough?" is not a question that can easily be answered. As human beings, we have different standards of living, net worths, and financial goals, and we can all still be in God's will, no matter our circumstances.

The Key Is Not "How Much?" But Rather, "How Much Is Enough for Me?"

During the Christmas giving challenge, James and Silas didn't struggle with how much to give because Landon and I, as their parents, were giving them the funds—though James did wonder if the funds could be used for a new Nintendo Switch. As our boys age and mature, they will ask themselves questions about how much to give. As they walk into adulthood and begin to create a financial roadmap (hopefully with one of their goals being radical generosity!), they will also wrestle with the question, "How much is enough for me?"

This is a question I've asked myself in my personal life, and as a financial advisor, I often see clients who desire to maximize kingdom impact while wrestling with this thought-provoking and vital question.

Uh, okay, Bethany, you may be thinking. *I'm on board—at least to consider this question—but it feels big. Enormous. Daunting. So how do I figure it out?*

I'm so glad you asked!

Thankfully, God gives us some helpful guidelines to think through as we grapple with this question.

We are not to be lazy and slothful (Proverbs 24:30-34), but we are to work with all our hearts at what God has called us to do (Colossians 3:23-24).

The example of work ethic that Paul set for the Thessalonians was in order to not be a burden to them, and he reminded them, "For even when we were with you, we used to give you this order: If anyone is not willing to work, then he is not to eat, either" (2 Thessalonians 3:10 NASB).

Providing for yourself and if applicable, your family, is God's minimum and maximum when it comes to determining how much is enough.

Work should not be taken to an extreme and justified by our misuse or misinterpretation. We should balance the priorities God has laid down in His Word in relation to Him, our job, serving at church, volunteer opportunities, responsibilities to family or children, and much more.

Psalm 127:2 is one of my favorite verses on the subjects of work and rest. *The Message* reads, "It's useless to rise early and go to bed late, and work your worried fingers to the bone. Don't you know he enjoys giving rest to those he loves?"

Let me repeat that for those of us in the back—you know, the Marthas in the room, not the Marys. "Don't you know he enjoys giving rest to those he loves?"

While the work God has called me to vocationally is one of the greatest joys of my life, it's very easy for me to forget that He also wants to give me rest. Not just sleep. *Rest.* I recognize that we rest when we sleep, but there is a difference between sleep and rest. I'm a great sleeper but I am terrible at resting. And I'll bet many reading this book struggle with it as well. It's critical to carve out times when we're not sleeping, but resting our minds and spending time in solitude or with loved ones or friends.

Scripture reminds us, "Do not weary yourself to gain wealth, cease from your consideration of it. When you set your eyes on it, it is gone. For wealth certainly makes itself wings like an eagle that flies toward the heavens" (Proverbs 23:4-5 NASB1995).

As we look at providing for ourselves, and if applicable, our family, we must determine the fine line between provision and protection.

We are to provide for our own needs and our family's needs, but not leave so much to them that they have no opportunity to trust God to work in their lives.

Providing for our families is different from hoarding. Hoarding wealth is the result of a basic lack of trust in God. Accumulation is an attempt to make sure we are protected and have enough for the future. However, a real issue that can present itself is that we may not be convinced that God will continue to supply all our needs as He has promised (Philippians 4:19). We attempt to help God out. And many of us struggle with this.

Instead, Jesus told us to store up treasures in heaven and not here on earth (Matthew 6:19-21). The writer of Ecclesiastes observed, "There is a grievous evil which I have seen under the sun: riches being hoarded by their owner to his hurt" (Ecclesiastes 5:13 NASB1995).

But in verses 19-20, we also find that God is not opposed to us enjoying the fruits of our labor. If God has given us riches and wealth (which is simply having more than we need), it is a gift from Him, and it is to be received and enjoyed as such. The key is to learn to enjoy it with God's blessing. Learn to enjoy and use the gift according to God's desires and not according to the ways of the world.

When we prove ourselves faithful with what God has given us, He will then entrust us with more (Matthew 25:21, 23). How are we to be faithful in using material blessings? One demonstration is to give freely to the Lord's work.

When someone is in need, we are not commanded to wish that they be clothed and fed. Instead, we are instructed to provide them with what they lack (James 2:14-16; 1 John 3:17-18). As we sow these good seeds, God will supply more seed, and "you will be enriched in every way to be generous in every way, which through us will produce thanksgiving to God" (2 Corinthians 9:11 ESV; see also verses 8-15).

The Dead Sea is dead because water cannot flow out from it—it takes in but does not give out. The Sea of Galilee, on the other hand, is full of life because it is a channel—as its water flows out, it is replenished with a fresh supply. In the same way, we are to be channels of God's blessing so that His life may flow through us to others.

All in all, the key is to have balance and spend time with God to determine what that balance should be. You may desire to pray as Agur did in Proverbs 30:8-9, "[God] give me neither poverty nor riches...That I not be full and deny You and say 'Who is the Lord?' or that I not be in want and steal, and profane the name of my God" (NASB1995).

Living an Open-Handed Life

My longtime client, Kim, is a powerful example of sacrificially asking, "How much is enough for me?"

Every December, I eagerly await Kim's email that I confidently know will arrive. In fact, I have a reminder set to reach out to Kim each year, but thus far, in the years I've served her, a reminder has never been needed.

And sure enough, like clockwork, this past December, Kim's annual email popped into my inbox. It never gets old. With excitement, I double clicked on the message, already knowing the gist of what the words would say.

The emails read something like this, "Dear Bethany, Merry Christmas! I hope you are well and enjoying this season. As usual, I'd like to know if I have gains in my investment accounts that I could charitably give before the end of the year. Please take all the gains and place them in my donor-advised fund. I'm prayerfully asking the Lord what ministries He desires me to bless, and I can't wait to see what He has in store!"

Kim decided a long time ago, as we developed a personal finish line for her and answered the question "How much is enough for me?," to evaluate her accounts toward the end of each calendar year. At that time, she would give away anything above the finish line amount. This is a great example of prayerfully and thoughtfully considering this very important question and taking action in a way that works well for Kim's specific circumstances.

Retirement God's Way

For many of us, thinking through this finish-line question also ties into a question of retirement.

Hebrews 12:1 says, "Let us run with endurance the race that is set before us" (ESV).

So what does this verse mean in relation to the subject of retirement, especially since the Bible is virtually silent on the subject of retirement? Scripture makes no mention of ceasing work at age 60 or 65.

I believe it means if we feel God's leading and are in a financial position (or our health requires us) to change the nature of our activity in God's kingdom, that's wonderful, but we should never be motivated to stop producing fruit. If God has called us to end a season of working years, then He is surely calling us to a new season with new purpose.

There's never a point, as Christians, when we sigh and say, "Well, all done here. I'm going to sit back and do nothing." My friend, many times, later seasons of life are when we have the most capacity, the most resources, and the most wisdom to pour into others for Jesus' work. We don't stop serving the Lord until our last breath leaves our body, and we are reunited with Him.

With proper planning, we can have the financial freedom to use our talents and abilities to fulfill God's next leg of our unique journey. Here are a few questions to consider if you are thinking through a retirement decision:

1. Should I retire from my current occupation?
2. How does retiring from this occupation help me fulfill God's purpose in my life?

3. When should I retire?
4. How will I continue to provide for myself (and my family, if applicable)?
5. What will I do next? What am I retiring *to*?

Retirement is simply the start of the next phase of service in God's kingdom.

At Blue Trust, we love learning from Ron Blue, the founder of our firm. While Ron is no longer involved in the day-to-day operations of Blue Trust, hearing his wisdom in this area and many others helps us refocus on what we're called to do and steward our entire lives for the kingdom.

In an article originally published on the Ron Blue Institute website, Ron writes:

> I often get asked the question: "how much is enough?" This question resonates deeply with me. In the mid 1970s, after I first became a Christian, I was involved in an evangelistic campaign through Campus Crusade for Christ. I worked all day at the large accounting firm I had started, and then I headed to a small rented space at night to work the phones at a metal desk in a creaky chair. During that time, my heart was captured by the hope of the gospel, and the perspective I attained in the evenings spent with Campus Crusade changed my view of my "day job."
>
> From that point on in my life, I was riveted by the truth that perspective has everything to do with contentment, and prosperity has very little to do with it. Those busy, successful days often left me frustrated and empty;

while the meaningful evenings spent engaged in evangelism left me hungry for more. Contentment, it turned out, had nothing to do with how much money I made or who I played golf with. It had everything to do with joining God in what He was doing in the world.

"How much is enough?" is a question that a financial planner spends most of his days helping people to answer. Budgets, retirement planning, debt repayment, college savings, insurance needs, etc., all are various ways of answering that question with a client.

My financial advice over the years has been to "set finish lines." Decide ahead of time where you want or need to end up in various financial areas, and then work out a plan to head in that direction. Decide on your long-term goals first. Then, determine the margin you will need in order to save for those goals. Finally, set a spending plan that will give you the margin you desire so that you can meet the long-term goals. Financially and materially, this is my ongoing advice in various forms to the many questions I've encountered from clients.

Spiritually, though, the true answer to "how much is enough?" has much more to do with contentment and perspective than it does with 401(k)s and budgets. We will always be constrained by an earthly perspective with earthly temptations and concerns, but in His Word, God gives us a glimpse into eternity. By meditating on Scripture and using it as a touchstone for our souls when we are tempted to be anxious about our material provision, we are capable of re-focusing our perspective and becoming free to be content—whatever we have. I encourage you to put yourself in the path of perspective-altering opportunities. Whether that means that you spend time in Bible Study,

> participate in service in your community, join with missionaries by supporting their service, or even take a walk in a garden and appreciate the completely non-material beauty of a flower, your life will be enriched by the process of seeking an eternal perspective on a regular basis.[1]

What do you think? I know, I know. It seems a bit drastic—maybe even a little scary. Maybe even a lot scary. I sigh; and sometimes, I cry because this concept overwhelms me too. Or I feel distrustful, even though I've experienced God's faithfulness again and again in the past. But I know that asking the question, "How much is enough for me?" is crucial to being a lifelong steward of all God has entrusted to me.

And just as the Holy Spirit led Ron to find contentment, showed Kim how to give sacrificially, and allowed my parents to be a part of kingdom work as they answered the question "How much is enough for our family?", the Holy Spirit also speaks to you and to me.

For me, it sounds something like, "Dear One, you can trust Me. I know your situation. Think of My faithfulness in your past. I hold you in the palm of My hand. And I desire for you to run after Me with all your heart, living a life of complete submission and surrender. You can trust Me. You *can* trust Me. And when you wonder, again, *you* can trust *Me*."

8

Your Future, God's Way

Living a Life of Values-Based Hope

Holding the screen door back with one foot, I pushed the heavy front door open. It creaked as I stepped inside. The house smelled like it always had. Grandma's cooking, wood paneling, Christmases past, cousins, chocolate chip cookies, and so much more. I closed my eyes as my senses were overwhelmed with special memories. Heavy gold drapes still hung from the windows as I stepped from the entryway linoleum onto the heavily padded off-white carpet of the formal living room—otherwise known as the Christmas tree room.

Each year, Cousin Amy and I would share the same oversized chair to open our gifts together. The three sisters-in-law would convene on the couch. Grandma and Grandpa had their special seats on either side of us, and my dad and his two brothers would sit on chairs dragged in from the dining room. Cousins and presents everywhere. Wrapping paper littered the floor. Laughter and joy and chaos consumed us. These memories washed over me as I walked in, along with the smell, and I thought about how some things never change…and yet, everything changes.

I'd visited my grandparents many times since I was born. I stayed with them while my parents traveled, too many times to count. Padding down the hallway early in the morning, just a little girl in my nightgown, drawn in by the smell of strong coffee, aftershave, and my grandpa's deep voice saying, "Good morning, Sweetie!" in an enthusiastic way that made me confident I was special. He was always reading his Bible when I walked in. Grandma would be in her robe, cooking flat eggs (my own special name for her signature scrambled eggs), toast, and bacon. And we would sit down together and eat our breakfast. I was safe and loved.

Years ago, when Grandpa died at age 90, he'd experienced many challenges in that final year. His lungs just couldn't get healthy, and we'd watched him go downhill. I arrived in town the night before he died, because we knew it was close to the end of his life. By then, he was in a nursing home because of the round-the-clock care he required, and I remember wishing I could sing hymns to him and just stay by his side.

But I didn't. I left, ignoring the tug on my heart to remain.

He died that night, and I will remember from now on to do what the Lord impresses on my heart. Sometimes you don't get a second chance. Grandpa's funeral was an incredible remembrance of his life. He lived a full life—with ups and downs, victories and failures, and some deep pain like all of us experience. It was a life well-lived, which he lived for the glory of the Lord.

God graciously left Grandma with us for a number of years after Grandpa passed away, and then He took her home to heaven as well. She was 97, and she and Grandpa truly left a legacy.

As I walked out of the Christmas tree room, I quickly found the dimmer switch on the wall that turned on the light over the dining room table. It clicked on easily, and I stopped, stunned, as the room came into focus. I looked at the china cabinet with Grandma's beautiful display (in fact, I accidentally chose the same fine china pattern when I married Landon). And then I couldn't help but stare at all the empty chairs.

The same dining table I always remembered, the same chairs, and the same upholstery. Now the room was empty, dim, and silent. And I thought of laughter. So much laughter. Grandpa and Grandma at the ends of the table. Grandma closer to the kitchen so that she could refill sweet teas and waters, and retrieve dessert when it was time.

The dining room table was the adults' table. I pictured my dad and his two brothers, sitting with their wives, laughing and talking, catching up, and eating delicious food—usually roast, gravy, potatoes and carrots, garden peas, sometimes Jell-O salad, and homemade rolls. I sat around the corner at the kids' table. But sometimes, if an adult couple was missing, I would sit at the big table or on an old brown stool that was added. I always sat by Grandpa, and he always held my hand tightly in his.

And on this night of his passing, I knew the table was the same, the chairs were the same, the room was the same, and the smell was the same. And yet, everything changed. People who formerly sat at this table regularly were no longer with us. Full of so much life here on earth, but, as James wrote in James 4:14, also just a vapor. How can it be? This is truly a mystery we cannot understand.

Each of us, whether we recognize it or not, is leaving a legacy. Legacy is simply defined as how we are remembered when we are gone. As my grandparents left memories and impressions engraved on my heart, their encouragement, beliefs, and actions helped mold me into the woman God has called me to be today. We all hold a sacred responsibility of pouring into others for Jesus.

Psalm 145:4 says, "One generation commends your works to another; they tell of your mighty acts." It's a high calling to know we are responsible for pouring into generations to come.

In my work with clients, I have found a common theme when

legacy discussions arise. Many of us believe a lie from Satan that says if our lives don't look a certain way, we don't leave a legacy. As if God forgot to include us in the legacy-leaving privileges and responsibilities. We don't count, and our possible legacy doesn't matter.

Maybe you had hoped to marry, but at this point in time, God hasn't brought a mate into your life. You keep waiting, and it feels like life would really be able to take off—God could start using you for His glory—if you could just find that perfect match. Then, you could be a godly influence and would have a powerful legacy to leave.

Maybe you are married and had hoped to have children, but that dream simply hasn't been realized. You've tried for years, but to no avail. You've cried out to God, and yet, nothing. I mean, the world repeats the lie that if you don't have children, there is no one to carry on your legacy. Are they right?

Maybe you were married, and your marriage ended with a word you hoped would never enter your vocabulary—*divorce*. You prayed for years. Heartbreaking years on your knees with many tears. You try not to believe what you know is a lie, but Satan whispers that this word defines you. This is who you'll always be. Who would desire *your* influence?

Maybe you are married, and your husband is not a believer. Or he says he's a believer but doesn't seem to live a godly life. You've prayed for years that he would experience a breakthrough with Jesus, but so far, it hasn't happened. I mean, what could God do with you alone, when all you've desperately prayed for and desired is to be a team? Surely, you can't impact lives for generations to come on your own. Another lie.

Maybe you're married, with adult children, and those children are prodigals. They aren't seeking Jesus' best for their lives in this season. Your white picket fence picture with grandchildren and bushy azaleas hasn't happened, and you battle jealousy as Christmas cards from friends arrive by mail with their large photos of seemingly perfect families. Isn't it impossible to leave a legacy if your adult kids don't seem to want anything but your money?

Do any of these scenarios hit close to home? For many of us, when we see the word *legacy*, our brains turn off automatically as our subconscious whispers, "Ah, you don't have a legacy to leave. How ridiculous for you to even think you'd have something of value to pass to future generations. It's a waste to even think about that."

I pray, in Jesus' name, that you rebuke the enemy when you hear these messages. These are lies from the pit of hell.

Your life matters no matter the roles God has called you to or the situations you find yourself in.

Your life matters because you are made in God's image, and God has called you to a purpose and has given you great plans.

The fact is, we will all leave a legacy, and the decisions we make during our lifetime will end up determining our ultimate legacy.

The legacy you leave is vital for the continuance and growth of the body of Christ. Merriam-Webster's defines the word *vital* as: "concerned with or necessary to the maintenance of life."[1] It's necessary. It's a must. It's a nonnegotiable. Just as we've discussed throughout our time together, if you don't stand confidently with purpose in the plans God has for you, not only are you going to miss out, but the rest of us will miss out as well.

Iron Sharpens Iron and *Ezer Kenegdo*

Over the years, as I've grown in responsibility at my job, the concept of leaving a legacy has broadened into so much more than I originally understood or anticipated.

About five years ago, I volunteered to lead a group at Blue Trust for a program called Iron Sharpens Iron. Every few years, we begin Iron Sharpens Iron again to assimilate newer team members into small groups for learning and discipleship. Think of a church small group but with a professional aspect added in. These groups are ideal for eager and unseasoned financial planners who desire to be on an advisor career track.

I was pumped when I found out I'd been graciously allowed to lead one of these small groups. I have a passion for pouring into my Blue Trust family, and I've experienced times of aloneness in my professional life when I desperately wished there had been someone to come alongside me in an authentic way—lowering walls of ego and image—to simply be real together. I felt confident my new Iron Sharpens Iron group had the potential to become a safe community, and I couldn't wait to receive the names of my new group members.

On an unassuming Monday morning, my group list popped into my email inbox, and as I read through the names, I was paralyzed—my right hand on my computer mouse, my eyes locked on the bright laptop screen, and my heart in my throat. An unexpected twist in my plan had arisen, and I wasn't sure if I could still lead this newly formed team.

Why?

All six people assigned to my group were men.

I was the leader, and I was to lead men.

Young men who were just starting out in their careers. Incredibly bright young men with deep spiritual maturity who were enthusiastic about their hopeful futures at Blue Trust.

My sudden paralysis had nothing to do with the actual people in the group. I already knew the people were rockstars.

It only had to do with me.

I can't lead men! I wailed in my own mind as, alone in my office, my eyes filled with tears.

"I wasn't made to lead men," I told Jesus as I began to pray. "I only feel comfortable leading women. That's my lane."

Abruptly, something I'd been over-the-moon excited about became a pit in my stomach as I focused on how unqualified and inept I was to lead a team of young men.

I moved on with my Monday, as usual, but a heavy spirit of discouragement hovered over me. I let the enemy gain a foothold in my heart, and I became consumed with what I "couldn't" do, how I "wasn't" equipped, and how I felt certain this assignment must be a mistake.

Monday afternoon, as I worked diligently on a financial plan, I continued to feel distracted and distraught. I took a break and walked downstairs into the kitchen from my home office. As I mindlessly turned on the Keurig, pulled out the Original Donut Shop Snickers coffee pod, and placed it into the machine, I decided it might be a good idea to ask Jesus what He thought. That may seem obvious to you, but so many times, I become extremely consumed with myself—my thoughts, my inadequacies, my concerns—and I don't immediately turn to God to see what He has to say about it. You know, the actual sovereign author of life, Scripture, and all things eternal.

As I placed my Easter bunny mug onto the base of the coffee maker, I spoke aloud.

"Lord, You know I was excited about this opportunity, and now look what's happened. I'm scared, and I don't want to do this anymore. Will You show me what You want me to do?"

Ezer kenegdo.

Immediately, these two words popped into my head. I slowly spoke the words out loud to our dog George, who was eagerly waiting beside me in the kitchen, hoping I'd drop a morsel of anything he could devour.

And yes, I said *ezer kenegdo* aloud with my strong southern twang. I don't know how to properly pronounce Hebrew words. I mean, I grew up in the panhandle of Florida, basically lower Alabama, for crying out loud.

My pronunciation didn't matter a bit to George, or the Lord, as my eyes filled with tears—yet again in the same day—and I knew God was reminding me of a truth He'd shared with me in the past.

In Genesis 2:18, the Bible tells us God said, "It is not good for the man to be alone; I will make him a *helper suitable for him*" (NASB, emphasis added).

Now, how many of us have heard that exact scripture more times than we can count?

I know I have.

And it always seemed like *helper* meant a demure, soft-spoken subordinate. In my mind, it even meant someone wimpy, boring, flat, and disappointing.

Guess what?

That's not what *helper* means here.

These are God's first words about women—who we are, what our purpose is, our destiny, our future, all wrapped up in this phrase *helper suitable for him,* or in Hebrew, *ezer kenegdo*. Do you know what that means?

Get ready, because it's exciting.

It doesn't mean a helper who is soft, boring, and demure.

It means lifesaver.

Life-giver.

Strength and power.

Warrior.

The word *ezer* is a military term. It's used around 20 other times in the entire Old Testament. In most instances the person being described is God Himself—when His people desperately needed Him to come through for them.

Here are some other examples of God as helper: "I lift up my eyes to the mountains—where does my help [*ezer*] come from?" (Psalm 121:1). And, "There is no one like the God of Jeshurun, who rides on the heavens to help [*ezer*] you" (Deuteronomy 33:26).

And on that Monday afternoon, I desperately needed this reminder—that men and women hold equal value and dignity in

God's eyes. When God talks about us as women, He's talking about an equal partner, not a demure and disappointing helper.

We, as women, so many times—in fact, I would say most of the time—don't give ourselves enough credit. We stand back, timid and uncertain, and we don't step forward into the destiny God has for us. We experience unique challenges that men don't understand or experience, just as men experience challenges that we don't understand. Because God crafted us differently, uniquely, and *on purpose*, precious ladies. On purpose to make a difference for His kingdom.

If you've wondered if you could step forward at school, work, church, or in any area of your personal life, the answer is 100 percent, yes.

Absolutely!

When I wondered if I could lead this Blue Trust Iron Sharpens Iron group, I didn't immediately see the truth. But, of course I could lead this group! I just needed a gentle reminder of two words: *ezer kenegdo*.

Can we really step out of our comfort zones to make an impact? To leave a legacy?

The answer is a wholehearted yes.

If God has called you, He will equip you. You are an *ezer kenegdo*—a life-giving, gifted, and highly favored image-bearer of the one true God. Women have an irreplaceable role to play. God has gifted us with fierce devotion, an ability to suffer great hardships and keep moving, and a vision to make the world a better place.

Without *you*, dear sister, much will be lost. Without your belief in what the Lord can do through you and your willingness to leave a legacy for Jesus—no matter your life situation—people will miss out. We are set apart, believed in, invited, valued, of immeasurable worth, and blessed.

And one more characteristic we embody through Christ: We are *brave*. Being a warrior looks like bravery, and sometimes, bravery doesn't look like we imagine. I envision bravery as storming a castle to rescue someone (and I don't even like to sweat), but bravery can also look like giving ourselves grace. That's brave. Allowing ourselves to rest. That's brave. Believing in the gifts God has given us. That's brave. Knowing that if we're going through a season of struggle, it's okay to talk to a counselor or other safe person. That's *really* brave. Bravery can take different forms in each of us and in different seasons.

Sister, let's not walk with our heads down quietly. Let's rally and encourage each other to know that God has a very special and specific purpose for us, and I want to fulfill every ounce of that purpose while I'm here on this earth. And a big part of that purpose is pouring into others to leave a legacy.

What Does a Legacy Look Like?

So if we're all on different journeys, called to different roles and responsibilities, and God has called us all to leave a legacy, what exactly does that legacy look like? Practically, how do you do it?

Let's start by asking ourselves the following questions:

1. If someone were to follow me around for a day or a week, what would that person conclude is of value and gain to me?
2. In today's society, why is it so difficult to think in terms of the eternal (as opposed to the temporal)?
3. In what ways might focusing intentionally on leaving a godly legacy affect my day-to-day life?
4. How can I purposefully invest in spiritual and social capital?

At Blue Trust, we often teach our clients to think through three types of capital we can use to invest in others.

Financial capital is money and material assets like land, stock, and jewelry.

Social capital is the character qualities necessary to be effective and productive in society. Qualities like work ethic, punctuality, integrity, and honesty.

Spiritual capital is understanding the truth of God's Word and being able to apply it. It's recognizing there are biblical absolutes; knowing how to accept Christ, walk by faith, and trust God; and understanding the biblical principles of money management, parenting, and relationships.

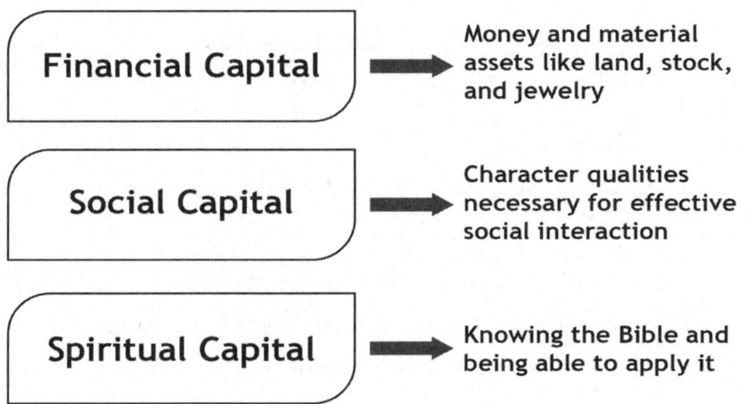

As Jesus followers, part of leaving a legacy is building spiritual and social capital in others. If we come to the end of our lives and have amassed financial capital but let spiritual and social capital fall by the wayside, we've missed out on the opportunity to fully pour out all we could have. Furthermore, the financial capital accumulated will be of no value if the other forms of capital are not present. Building social and spiritual capital in others takes intentionality to live a balanced life so that we build space for quality time and important conversations.

The Message renders Ephesians 5:11-17 this way:

> Don't waste your time on useless work, mere busywork, the barren pursuits of darkness. Expose these things for

> the sham they are. It's a scandal when people waste their lives on things they must do in the darkness where no one will see. Rip the cover off those frauds and see how attractive they look in the light of Christ.
>
> Wake up from your sleep,
> Climb out of your coffins;
> Christ will show you the light!
>
> So watch your step. Use your head. Make the most of every chance you get. These are desperate times!
>
> Don't live carelessly, unthinkingly. Make sure you understand what the Master wants.

These verses encourage us as we consider what kind of legacy we should desire to leave. We're encouraged to watch our steps, use our heads for wisdom, and to make the most of every chance we have to influence others for Jesus.

As women of worth, we desire to be women who are pure in heart, intentional, trustworthy, content, hardworking, sacrificial, wise in making business decisions, and more. When we rely on the Lord to continue refining and growing our faith, only then will we mature as believers and truly leave a legacy that will ripple throughout generations for Jesus.

Russ Crosson, our chief mission officer at Blue Trust, describes this refinement and intentionality by saying, "A life well spent is a life that earns and uses money to 'buy' time to balance life in order to impact people to be productive and godly members of society. It is a life that focuses on the eternal in the realm of the temporal so that at the end of life we will have been found faithful with what God considers important."[2]

As we seek the Lord's face to consider our influence on those around us, I pray we feel no pressure, no shame for past mistakes, no regret of what "could" have been. Instead, I pray we are filled with hope as we seek, with great anticipation, to join God in what He's already doing in the world around us. I pray we intentionally ask the Father how He desires for us to pour social and spiritual capital into others as we watch our steps, use our heads, and make the most of every chance we get. We are *ezer kenegdos*, with a one-of-a-kind and irreplaceable calling to live out.

9

You Have What It Takes

Embodying Who You Long to Be

I fought with my navy golf umbrella as the deluge of rain attempted to drown me in the parking lot of our local Mexican restaurant. The umbrella threatened to flip inside out as the wind fiercely blew. I looked around, wondering if I'd accidentally landed in the world of *The Wizard of Oz* and was actually in the middle of a Kansas tornado, but I didn't see Toto or Dorothy anywhere. Thankfully, I'd completed all my client interactions for the day, so it didn't matter that I now looked like a drowned rat while meeting my dear friend for dinner.

As I stepped onto the sidewalk by the restaurant's entrance, Melissa met me from inside and held the door open. Shivering from the cold, I shook rain off my umbrella while closing it. I was aggravated because my hair blossoms into an enormous mushroom when drying naturally.

Melissa shook her head and immediately burst out laughing, and so did I. We were both a mess! She motioned to the booth she'd already nabbed for us, and I slid onto the empty green cushion. I slipped off my wet high heels and curled my legs under me on the seat. After being soaked in a storm, I couldn't think of anything more soothing than chips and salsa, guacamole, and tortilla chicken soup. My stomach growled as I realized how hungry I was.

Just as she usually did when we met for a meal, Melissa reached across the table and grabbed my hand for a moment.

"Bethany, how are you...aside from drenched?" Melissa asked.

Before I spoke, I took a deep breath and laid my head back against the tall booth cushion. My mind flashed back to the meal Melissa and I shared together at this very restaurant about a year before this, when she'd seemed calm and unhurried, and I'd seemed, well, a wreck. It was during that meal when I finally became weary of just surviving. Of wondering if I belonged anywhere. Of being tired of being tired. Of doubting my value and purpose. Of wondering when everyone would realize I was an impostor in my own life—seemingly winning in every area, but in reality, I was a duck, paddling under the water at a frantic pace just to keep going.

A year ago seemed like forever. And also, like yesterday.

God had done so much.

I chose my words carefully as I readied myself to respond to Melissa's question.

"Melissa, I am abundantly at peace."

And I meant it. No frantic feet paddling underneath the surface of the water. No lip biting. No fidgeting.

"Soon after a conversation we had about a year ago, here at this very restaurant, I began a journey," I told her. "A journey inspired by the outflow of your own heart, Melissa. The way you trust the Lord to believe in who He says you are has always been such an inspiration to me. I never thought it was really possible to live out of who He says I am. But after some hard work over this past year, God is helping me get it. He's allowing me to see and experience more of who He is so that I can rest in who He's called me to be. And the most wonderful part is that as I've gained confidence in many areas of my life—from faith to finances to the various roles God has called me to as a woman. And, I've been able to begin pouring that confidence into the women I serve as clients. Encouraging them to begin their own journeys of discovery to truly live out of who God says they are."

I could see Melissa's eyes shining bright with tears. There was nothing I'd seen excite her more than a woman who is activated for Jesus and living with purpose.

You see, I'd believed lies for so long, that I didn't even realize they were lies. That's how sneaky lies can be. Lies like I would never be enough. I could never really belong. I would never confidently manage my finances. I could never deserve a seat at the table.

No matter what.

And my guess is that you sometimes struggle with these tricky falsehoods as well.

While the enemy would like for us to believe we're alone in our struggles, the fact is, we are not.

We are not alone, and God will equip us for what He's called us to do. Will storms rage around us? Sure they will. Will wind turn our umbrellas inside out and make us look like drowned rats? Sometimes. But take heart.

If we are believers in Jesus, we have the Holy Spirit living right inside of us. In Romans 8, the apostle Paul talks about the Holy Spirit interceding on our behalf with groanings we don't understand—so much power lies here, and many times, we underestimate this power. And because we choose not to plug in and acknowledge this sacred power in our lives that can lead us into all truth, we live lives of quiet resignation.

Remember *ezer kenegdo*? The one who comes through when you can't count on anyone else. The life-giver.

That's who we are when we're living out of who Christ says we are.

Is it easy?

Obviously not.

Does anyone, ever, just plain arrive?

Definitely not. This is a continuous journey in relationship with Jesus, battling it out every moment on this side of heaven.

Some days, I plug into the power, and I walk in who God has fully created me to be, shining for His glory.

Other days, I slink back into shadowy lies, letting the enemy have a foothold, and believing I'll never be enough.

In a season of learning to believe in who God says I am, I have clung to this verse in Psalm 65:11:

> You crown the year with a bountiful harvest; even the hard pathways overflow with abundance (NLT).

Who crowns the year? Oh, right. Not me. God does.

Who brings a bountiful harvest? Oh, yeah. Again, not me. God does.

Who makes the hard pathways overflow with abundance? Ah. Yep. God again.

So why do I believe it all depends on me then? If I wasn't so afraid of needles, ink, and something permanently being on my body that I can't remove, I would seriously tattoo this verse on my forehead.

I love this reminder of God's care for us. And He completely acknowledges we will walk hard pathways. Some of the paths aren't easy. They are hard. Sometimes heartbreakingly hard.

But they will be worth it. The journey will be worth it.

As we've journeyed through this book together, I pray you have gleaned new truths and principles to help you continue building a strong foundation of faith and finances. Practically, we've walked through tips and tools to equip us as we seek to take one next step toward confidence in our identity, purpose, faith, and our finances.

In summary:

- We've learned that money is a tool, a test, and a testimony; and we've recognized that money is not a measure of self-worth, a guarantee of contentment, a reward for godly living, or a measure of success.

- We now know how to help make money a nonissue when stewarding our finances by focusing on creating consistencies like carving out time for annual goal planning weekends, setting up a budgeting system that works for you, planning for the unexpected, and being intentional with the juggle of work and life balance.
- We've equipped ourselves to understand how to steward our financial everything, which starts with a willingness to engage in areas where we feel less confident.
- We've discovered how to do hard things, such as steer clear of debt and make wise investments.
- We've talked through how to begin a giving journey and how to take generosity to the next level by employing strategies like:
    - Creating a spontaneous-giving bucket
    - Creating and utilizing a giving grid
    - Opening a donor-advised fund
    - Giving appreciated assets
    - Bundling charitable giving
- We've prepared ourselves to teach the children in our lives—age appropriately—how to be excellent stewards of what God has entrusted to them.
- We learned to ask the question, "How much is enough for me?" while thinking through what retirement looks like God's way. We've asked ourselves wise questions as we prepare for a season of life with less or no earned income.
- We've been empowered by learning we are *ezer kenegdos*,

> life-givers with a high calling to leave a legacy for Jesus through our financial, spiritual, and social capital.

If you've ever doubted yourself, ask the Holy Spirit to remind you that you are an *ezer kenegdo*. A life-giver, called to His purposes.

If you've ever chosen a seat away from the conference table in a meeting, commit to choosing a seat around the table when the next work meeting arises. It's no accident you are in the room.

If you've ever restarted a budget over again, don't be afraid to jump in with the new strategies and tools you've learned in this book. You don't have to love spreadsheets to be successful with a budget.

If you've ever struggled to balance all the priorities of life and you've felt like you're constantly failing, remember, God will equip those He has called. The pressure is off of us. Your best is good enough. And He has given us the gift of rest, if we choose to prioritize it.

If you've ever thought of investments as a foreign language, think back to the sequential investment strategy stairsteps in chapter 4, and focus on one small step at a time. It's okay to ask for help if you need it.

Honesty check-in: Do I still want to hide in the closet and eat a Reese's once in a while? Good grief, yes. I'll pull you up a space on the carpet (if I move a pile of sweatshirts), and we'll eat some Reese's together.

I'm not saying that life is ever immediately and permanently sunshine and rainbows.

But I am saying 2 Peter 1:3 to both of us:

> His divine power has granted to us all things that pertain to life and godliness, through the knowledge of Him who called us to His own glory and excellence (ESV).

And I'm also reciting 2 Corinthians 5:17 to us:

> Anyone who belongs to Christ has become a new person. The old life is gone; a new life has begun! (NLT).

We've got it, dear friend. We've got the power. It's Jesus, and I can't wait to see how He empowers you to flip the switch, to recognize that we are truly women of worth. Would you be willing to just take one small step with me?

The bottom line is that with Jesus, we have what it takes.

Appendix A

Financial Planning with Purpose

In today's rapidly evolving financial landscape, more and more investors are seeking ways to align their investments with their personal values and beliefs. This shift is driven by a desire to find greater meaning in investing and to use capital as a force for good in the world. It's a powerful approach that brings your investments into alignment with what matters most to you.

As you explore the concept of values-based investing, here are two fundamental questions to ask yourself:

1. What kind of alignment do I desire?
2. What kind of impact do I want from my portfolio?

What Is the Difference Between Alignment and Impact?

Alignment is internally oriented and relates to your personal conscience and beliefs. It's about ensuring that your investments reflect your values and do not contradict your deeply held convictions. Do you want to avoid investing in companies involved in certain industries or practices? This method is about aligning your portfolio with your personal moral compass.

Impact, on the other hand, is external. It deals with the positive influence you want to have through your investment portfolio. Impact is about actively using your investments to help others and persuade change by directing capital toward causes that you care about.

We believe that being a faithful investor starts with one overarching principle—God owns it all (Psalm 24:1). Most Christians believe in that concept, but putting it into practice can be difficult. Until recently, values-based investment solutions were limited, often forcing investors to choose between financial returns and impact. This limitation hindered true personalization and often left investors feeling disconnected from their portfolios.

Impact Investing/Values-Aligned Investing

Traditionally, investors faced two primary choices:

1. Investing solely for financial return, or
2. Donating to charity to make a difference

Today, there's a powerful third option: impact investing or values-aligned investing. This approach seeks to generate both financial returns and positive change simultaneously. It's not a compromise but a force multiplier that allows you to grow your wealth, have a positive influence, and amplify your future giving potential. Values-based investing no longer requires sacrificing financial performance. You do not have to forfeit performance in order to align your portfolio with your values.

Instead, you are empowered with the ability to have a direct and immediate impact with your investment dollars, all while still meeting your personal financial goals.

Six Key Principles of Financial Planning

1. Understand that God owns it all (Psalm 24:1).
2. Begin with the end in mind (Proverbs 16:9).
3. Spend less than you earn (Proverbs 21:20).
4. Avoid the use of debt (Proverbs 13:11; 22:7).
5. Be generous (1 Timothy 6:17-19).
6. Diversify investments (Ecclesiastes 11:2).

Five Questions to Ask Yourself

If you can answer "yes" to each question below, you're probably on a solid financial track. If you answer "no" or "I don't know," you have some work to do in those areas.

1. Do you have written goals driving your financial decisions?
2. Are you giving, saving, and spending with purpose?
3. Are you making wise investments?
4. Are you on track as you save for the future?
5. Are you prepared for the impact of death or disability upon you and/or your family?

Questions to Ask a Potential Financial Advisor

1. How Will You Be Compensated?

It is wise to begin by asking how your financial advisor receives payment—through product commissions, fees, or hybrid—and understand that conflicts of interest can exist with different compensation models. Fee-only advisors are only compensated by fees paid from the client to the advisor, while commission-based advisors earn income from the products they sell to the client or the accounts they open. It's important to note that many fee-only financial professionals also act as a legal fiduciary, which means they are required by law to always put their client's best interests first. Commission-based financial professionals' duty lies with their employing brokers or dealers. It is not always easy to find this information. The advisor or their company may give you clues on their website or in their materials. If not, there are two separate governing bodies that may also help you find the answer.

Most investment companies (non-trust companies) are governed by the Securities and Exchange Commission (SEC), and the Financial Industry Regulatory Authority (FINRA) is the organization that helps regulate most individuals that are registered and licensed to sell or advise on investment products. The keyword is *most*. To research these advisors or advisory firms, use FINRA's Broker Check tool to see what licenses or certifications the advisor holds, which can give insight into how they are compensated. For example, the Series 6 and Series 7 allows someone to sell investment products for a commission, so a financial advisor with these licenses would likely earn commission-based income.

2. What Will Your Company Provide?

It is wise to learn more about a company's primary focus and philosophy. Every company has a lens through which they see the world.

In the financial world, offering proprietary financial products typically means more financial reward for the company selling them. In other words, some companies sell complex financial products in order to receive higher financial compensation. It is important to determine if these products actually perform better than standard products and if they come with higher fees.

Proprietary products can cost more and may be more complicated. Be sure to take the time to fully understand the details of a proprietary product before purchasing it.

Another alternative is to look for a financial advisor who offers objective, fee-only advice and is therefore not compensated based on the products they recommend. Many investors find it helpful to have a like-minded financial advisor who aligns closely with their goals and values.

3. What Are Your Credentials?

The financial industry is loaded with an alphabet soup when it comes to credentials and certifications. Therefore, sometimes it's difficult to determine which credentials mean what. FINRA alone references 200 professional designations.

A good rule of thumb is to choose an expert in their particular field. For instance, if you are looking for tax advice, it is preferable to choose a Certified Public Accountant (CPA) because of the high level of training and experience they have received. If you are looking for holistic financial advice, a CERTIFIED FINANCIAL PLANNER® (CFP®) certificant is often a wise choice because they are skilled in multiple areas of finance and have passed rigorous testing to obtain this designation.

4. Are You a Fiduciary?

What is a fiduciary advisor? At the most basic level, a fiduciary is required by law to have the customer's best interest as the primary focus above everything else pertaining to financial advice and recommendations. Fiduciary advisors legally cannot put their interests above the customer's. For example, they cannot recommend a financial product that is more costly when there is another one available that accomplishes the same goal at a lower cost.

As a trust company, Blue Trust is governed by the Tennessee Department of Financial Institutions (TDFI) and is required to follow the highest fiduciary standard. Most companies' websites will tell you if they are a fiduciary or not, or you can ask your financial advisor.

5. Do You Share My Values?

Growing your assets may be one of your investment goals, but you probably have other financial goals in mind as well. Perhaps you are hoping to fund or participate in mission work, support your local community and church, or pass down your wealth responsibly to the next generation. There are very specific conversations with your spouse and family that should take place as you prepare for retirement and beyond—especially if passing down your values is also important to you. For many people, the Bible offers clear direction for this process. Many Blue Trust advisors have obtained their Certified Kingdom Advisor® (CKA®) designation, which involves a certification process incorporating biblical principles into financial planning and investing.

It is often difficult to find wise counsel in a fallen world. Jesus did not say that following Him would be easy, but we know following Him is worth it. By taking the extra time and effort to seek wise counsel, we can increase our chances of stewarding His resources well.

At Blue Trust, we seek to be faithful stewards of all that is entrusted to us. If you would like our help, we are ready to serve. Please don't hesitate to contact us at info@bluetrust.com or 1-800-987-2987.

Appendix B

Precepts for Giving

From Chapter 5

1. Giving is a tangible way to acknowledge the ultimate ownership and provision of the sovereign God in our lives (see 1 Corinthians 4:7; Deuteronomy 8:16-18; Haggai 2:8; Psalms 24:1; 50:10-11).

2. We show honor and obedience to God in our giving. God commands us to give (see Proverbs 3:9-10; 1 Timothy 6:17-19; Luke 6:38).

3. Charitable giving is done in order to help prioritize the issues of life. Giving breaks the power of money (see Luke 16:11-13; Proverbs 18:10-11; Luke 12:33-34; 1 Timothy 6:9-10).

4. Charitable giving is done to meet the needs of others (see Exodus 16:18; 2 Corinthians 8:15; 9:12-14; Deuteronomy 15:10-11; Philippians 4:16; 1 John 3:17).

5. We draw personal rewards from the act of giving (see Revelation 22:12; 2 Corinthians 5:10; Matthew 6:20; Luke 12:33; Philippians 4:17; Matthew 16:27; 1 Corinthians 3:8-14).

6. Giving is an expression of worship and gratitude (see John 3:16; Romans 12:1; 2 Corinthians 8:1-6).

Appendix C

Financial Wisdom for Children:

What to Teach Young Children

✓ **Introduce the value of money.** Explain that money is how you pay for things. Maybe play pretend store or restaurant and demonstrate how you exchange money for goods.

✓ **Count coins together.** Teach children the different coin values and practice basic math number concepts.

✓ **Describe how people earn money through using their skills or providing a service.** Consider giving an allowance appropriate for your child's age and tied to household chores.

✓ **Set up three piggy banks or jars to help kids visually see how to divide their money for different purposes.** We recommend giving, saving, and spending.

✓ **Explain why it is important to live generously and**

help others. It is unwise to spend every penny you receive and have zero margin. Help children know that God calls us to be generous and meet the needs of others.

- ✓ **Share wisdom about spending decisions and the importance of tradeoffs.** Help children understand that money is limited and choices matter. By introducing the idea of tradeoffs early, they learn that saying "yes" to one thing often means saying "no" to something else.

- ✓ **Explain the wisdom of delayed gratification.** If your child wants an expensive item (or something you are not willing to pay for), encourage them to save for it. They may view the item differently when they must wait or spend their own money on it. If not and they still want to purchase it, help them buy the item and then celebrate their accomplishment together.

- ✓ **Use rewards to encourage wise giving, saving, and spending choices.**

- ✓ **Turn your weekly errands into teaching opportunities.** When visiting the bank, store, or ATM, explain how these places work and why you choose certain products (generic versus brand-name and sale versus non-sale items) or payment methods (cash, debit, credit, etc.).

Appendix D

Financial Wisdom for Children:

What to Teach Tweens and Teens

✓ **Help your kids find ways to begin earning money.** Tweens and teens can look for paid job opportunities at home or around the neighborhood, like dog walking, raking leaves, or mowing lawns. Consider having your teenagers help you with a yard sale. They can clean out their belongings and earn money while learning about pricing, sales, and hard work.

✓ **Explain to your children the importance of setting aside some of their earnings to tithe or help others. God calls us to share our riches and be wise stewards of the money entrusted to us.** Help your children choose a few charities that interest them. Perhaps, make it a family project to find out what the various organizations do, how well they accomplish their mission, and what percentage of the donations go to their cause. Then your children can decide where to donate their hard-earned dollars.

- ✓ **Remind kids of the importance of saving in order to reduce stress and create margin.** Consider matching their savings if they are working toward a certain goal (i.e., car, electronic device, camping equipment, etc.).

- ✓ **Educate your children on the basics of banking, debit cards, and credit cards.** Many banks offer kid-friendly checking accounts linked to parents' accounts, allowing tweens and teens to practice making deposits and purchases under parental supervision. Explain the differences between debit cards and credit cards and the dangers of repeatedly relying on credit.

- ✓ **Show your tweens and teens how to set up a budget and track their expenses.** Perhaps help them determine a budget for a certain amount of time (a week, a month, or three months) and track expenses during that time. At the conclusion, you can review the data together and help them decide what changes they may want to make to their spending plan. At the end of the day, the key to financial freedom is to spend less than you earn.

- ✓ **Take your kids shopping with you and explain how to compare prices, quality, and brands.** The grocery store is a great place to compare generic versus brand-name items and sale versus non-sale items. You can also show kids how to read unit labels on retail shelf price tags to easily compare the price of products. In addition, discuss wants versus needs and how unnecessary splurges, like gourmet coffees and subscription services, can add up quickly.

✓ **Consider paying your kids for reading financial books and providing a report to you.** Some suggested books are *Your Money Made Simple* by Russ Crosson, *Misbehaving* by Richard Thaler, *The Millionaire Next Door* by Thomas J. Stanley and William D. Danko, and *Psychology of Money* by Morgan Housel.

✓ **Help kids practice financial independence.** Gradually transition costs and responsibilities to your children throughout middle and high school so they can practice some financial independence while you are still close by to guide and support them.

Appendix E

Financial Wisdom for Children:

What to Teach Recent Graduates and Young Adults

✓ **Pray for your children and offer guidance, but allow them to find their own way, even through struggles. Adversity builds resilience and character.** Remind them that few people start in their dream job. Working hard to gain a better position or opportunity teaches valuable lessons and makes them more grateful for what they earn and accomplish. Young adults may struggle to realize they won't immediately match their parents' lifestyle, which took years of hard work to achieve.

✓ **Introduce the basics of investing.**

- What is a stock, bond, and mutual fund?
- What are the risks and rewards of each?
- Explain the power of compounding and why it's beneficial to start investing early in life.
- Address the importance of diversification, finding

a trustworthy financial advisor, and periodically monitoring your investments.
- Consider allowing them to experience investing by either providing a small amount of assets or utilizing a virtual investing simulation.

✓ **Ensure your children know how to:**
- Pay recurring and one-time bills.
- Apply for credit and manage it wisely.
- Plan for paying off debt (student loans, etc.).
- Save for future needs.

✓ **Intentionally and clearly state your expectations for your children after graduation, leaving no room for interpretation.** Can they stay in or move back into your home? If so, will they pay rent, and how much? How long can they live there? Are there requirements they must meet to live in your home? Though these may seem harsh, clearly defining how and for how long you'll help your child benefits both of you.

✓ **Remember the simple wisdom of give, save, and spend. Although their earnings have likely increased, they can still focus primarily on these main categories.**

Give: Encourage them to establish a plan to prioritize and practice generosity. Holding wealth with an open hand releases the power of money in our lives as we realize we are merely stewards of it.

Save: Show your children how to build an emergency fund and save for future investments and desires (down payment, new car, engagement ring, etc.). Teach them the importance of having liquidity for unexpected expenses or emergencies. Encourage them to take advantage of employer benefits, like matching 401(k) offerings.

Spend: Help them establish a budget that is in line with their income level. Teach them how to track income and expenses to ensure they are spending less than they earn. Guide them as they learn how to pay for the necessities of life (i.e., housing, gasoline, food, insurance) rather than just the items they want to pay for (i.e., gourmet coffee, clothing, upgraded technology). Life is about choices, and we spend money on what we value. Can I make the payments on that car? What rent amount can I afford? Let your children make these decisions. Allow them to learn the consequences of their choices—good or bad.

Acknowledgments

God is weaving a beautiful, unique tapestry in each of our lives. A design that can, at many times, appear messy and disorganized because we see each individual strand as it's being woven. Challenges are sewn in, blessings are stitched throughout, and perseverance, change, and growing in Jesus are faithfully and constantly woven through. As I think back to all God has done in my life to bring me to this Esther moment—"for such a time as this" (Esther 4:14)—I am humbled and stunned by His sovereignty and goodness. I am overwhelmed by the tapestry of grace He has so wholly woven into my life.

My first tapestry strand began with godly parents who have shown me how to live generously and stand on faith—even when it's hard. Thank you, Mom and Dad, Jim and Lynne Wise, for showing me what true generosity means and for building Jesus, and only Jesus, as the foundation in my life.

The next beautifully woven strand is my husband, Landon, and our deeply loved boys, James and Silas. Landon, I know you have made sacrifices to allow me to follow God's calling. Thank you for encouraging me and cheering me on. Thank you for the way you pour yourself out for others. I am amazed to think about the very (*very, very*) different personalities and giftings we have, and I am in awe that the Lord has made a way for us to minister together and spur each other on to love and good works. The impact you are making in your own arena will never be known on this side of heaven. I love you. And my sweet boys, James and Silas. Thank you for giving me an abundance of grace when my mind is scattered between work and family. I pray you will feel a clear and confident call from the Lord, as I have, to serve Him wholeheartedly and with excitement. God has great plans for both of you. Plans to prosper you and not to harm you. Plans to give you hope and a future. I am your number-one prayer warrior and biggest fan.

Much of my tapestry has threads of my Blue Trust family woven throughout, as well.

Russ Crosson, chief mission officer at Blue Trust, your deep and unwavering resolve to our company's mission continues to inspire me to dig into God's Word and never stop learning how to more effectively pour biblical financial advice into our clients. Our mission of helping Christians become financially free to assist in fulfilling the Great Commission is a mission I think about daily as I continue to learn from you and others at the firm. Thank you for your faithfulness to Jesus and the mission He has called us to.

Nick Stonestreet, former Blue Trust CEO, thank you for bringing a heart of acceptance and belonging to Blue Trust. Thank you for believing in women. Thank you for seeing a spark in me that I did not see in myself. I pray that spark will light a fire for Jesus and impact the world for His kingdom. You are a true world changer.

Brian Shepler, current Blue Trust CEO, how could I have ever imagined this is what God would do? That this would be His plan? You saw me at the very beginning of my Blue Trust journey. When I nearly ended the firm through a typo in an email, and when I made coffee for the entire office each morning after arriving at work; when I had no idea the plans God would have for us in future years. Thank you for always being an encouragement. Thank you for your willingness to support our first book written by a woman at Blue Trust!

Your stability, steadiness, humility, and hope in Jesus are inspiring. Blue Trust's greatest days are ahead with you at the helm.

Ruth Malhotra, Blue Trust's strategic partnerships manager, thank you for jumping on to our ship, even when I know you were terrified to take the leap. I will be forever grateful for the way you have poured into me, professionally and personally, as both a colleague and a friend. Thank you for inviting me to serve with you in our women's initiative efforts. You are a champion of women like no other!

Jeff Chinery, my boss and Everyday Steward division managing director, your belief in me and all the others you have supervised during your years at Blue Trust has marked each one of us forever. I have never known anyone like you. You foster a safe place to fail and offer a gentle invitation to grow and blossom. You have a gift of calling out in others what they don't yet see in themselves. You are a true gift to the kingdom of God and Blue Trust. Because of your quiet demeanor others may not realize it, but I will shout it from the mountaintops—You are a champion! And your belief in me has allowed Jesus to change my life in ways I never could have foreseen.

Sandy Morgan, former director of communications, and Malissa Light, senior communications specialist, thank you both for your encouragement and patience as we have walked this journey together. I know I cried during nearly every meeting as we discussed this project. It's because of the deep burden I feel from the Lord and my disbelief that He would allow me to author a book for Blue Trust. It still feels overwhelming! Your input has been invaluable, and your friendship is incredibly meaningful.

Our Blue Trust leadership team, thank you for trusting me to work on this project. Thank you for encouraging me to speak to women on Blue Trust's behalf. I do not take this responsibility or calling lightly, and I am committed to stewarding this God-given opportunity with humility and wisdom.

And God has woven in other strands.

Renown Publishing—Caleb Breakey, Steve Rzasa, Sara Ella, and Shannon Vandewaker—I am not being dramatic when I say I absolutely never could have written this book without your guidance, wisdom, coaching, editing, organizational skills, and belief in me. Each of you is called by God for a very special purpose at Renown. You are furthering His kingdom every day as you support and direct authors who desire to share their stories of God's love and faithfulness.

Harvest House Publishers, thank you for your willingness to work with me—a brand-new author! Thank you for your longtime relationship with Blue Trust and for your support of our mission.

As you can see, my tapestry has many colorful threads. Over the years, the threads seemed odd and out of place at times, but as God has uncovered and revealed *Women of Worth* in my mind and heart, each of the threads makes sense and has a vital place in the creation and heart of the book.

Dear reader, I pray you will know that God is weaving a tapestry of your own—a unique creation like no one else's—and in the seasons when the threads don't seem to make sense or you'd like to rip them out and start again, trust Him instead. Lean in. God has good plans prepared for you. And I cannot wait to see the tapestry He is weaving in you.

The inspiration behind my tapestry metaphor is from the poem "The Weaver" (often called "The Tapestry Poem") by Grant Colfax Tullar (1869–1950), an American minister, composer, and hymn writer.[1]

"The Weaver"

My life is but a weaving
Between my Lord and me;

I cannot choose the colors
He worketh steadily.

Oft times He weaveth sorrow
And I, in foolish pride,
Forget He sees the upper,
And I the under side.

Not til the loom is silent
And the shuttles cease to fly,
Shall God unroll the canvas
And explain the reason why.

The dark threads are as needful
In the Weaver's skillful hand,
As the threads of gold and silver
In the pattern He has planned.

He knows, He loves, He cares,
Nothing this truth can dim.
He gives His very best to those
Who chose to walk with Him.

Scripture Copyright Notifications

Notes

Chapter 2—Your Heart in Action

1. Anna Quindlen, *Loud and Clear* (New York: Ballantine Books, 2004), 11.

Chapter 3—You Are a Caretaker

1. Bank of America, "Women, Money, Confidence—A Lifelong Relationship," Bank of America (April 2024), 9, https://business.bofa.com/content/dam/flagship/workplace-benefits/id20_0905/documents/women-money-confidence.pdf.
2. Bank of America, "Women, Money, Confidence," 10.

Chapter 5—Your Life Overflowing

1. Alan Gotthardt, *The Eternity Portfolio* (Carol Stream, IL: Tyndale, 2003)

Chapter 6—You Lead the Way

1. Tim Kimmel, *Legacy of Love* (Portland, OR: Multnomah, 1989), 292.
2. "2024 Survey of the States," Council for Economic Education, accessed July 28, 2025, www.councilforeconed.org/policy-advocacy/survey-of-the-states/.

Chapter 7—You Are Called

1. Ron Blue, "How Much Is Enough?," Ron Blue Institute (January 31, 2017), https://ronblueinstitute.com/article/how-much-is-enough/. Used with permission.

Chapter 8—Your Future, God's Way

1. "Vital," Merriam-Webster.com, https://www.merriam-webster.com/dictionary/vital.
2. Russ Crosson, "Living a Life Well Spent," PowerPoint presentation.

Acknowledgments

1. Hans DePold, "Grant Tullar, Music Publisher," Bolton Historical Society—Bolton, Connecticut (August 11, 2006), https://boltoncthistory.org/grant-tullar-music-publisher/.